Book 3

Just Vocabulary

Intermediate

Includes Answer Key

Jeremy Harmer

Viva Books

New Delhi | Mumbai | Chennai | Kolkata | Bangalore | Hyderabad | Kochi | Guwahati

Text acknowledgements

pp7, 48, 61, 72, Macmillan English Dictionary for Advanced Learners by Michael Rundell and Gwyneth Fox, © Bloomsbury Publishing 2002. Reprinted by permission of Macmillan, Oxford; p13, Cambridge Learners' Dictionary © Cambridge University Press; pp18, 25, 31, 38, 42, 54, 68, Longman Dictionary of Contemporary English New Edition © Pearson Education Limited, 1978, 2003.

Photo acknowledgements

p8 ©Robert Llewellyn/Image State/Alamy; p15 ©Robert Llewellyn/Image State/Alamy; p22 © Alamy; p24 a and b ©Spectrum Colour Library, d, e and f ©Topham Picturepoint, c ©AC Waltham/Robert Harding Picture Library/Alamy; p31 top left and right ©Paul McMullin/Alamy, centre left and right ©Spectrum Colour Library, bottom left ©Peter Brooker/Rex Features, bottom right ©Topham Picturepoint, p32 ©image 100/Alamy; p40 ©Reeve Photography; p45 a and c © Corbis; b ©Rex Features; d ©Doug Scott/Powerstock; p60 a ©Braun Oral B; c and q ©Art Explosion Royalty Free; b f and i ©Sony UK; e ©Sharpe Electronics; all others ©Topham Picturepoint; p66 1 "Summer of The Seventeenth Doll", by Ray Lawler, First Published by Currency Press, Sydney Australia in 1978; 2 ©Hodder and Stoughton; 3 ©Topham Picturepoint, 4 ©Ronald Grant Archive; p68 ©Topham Picturepoint; p72 ©Popperfoto; p78 top right ©Erik Penozich/Rex Features; left ©Jon Feingersh/Corbis; bottom right ©Rex Features; p79 © b, e, g, h, i ©Topham Picturepoint, a, ©Dimitri Lundt/Corbis, c, ©Mitchell Gerber/Corbis, d, ©Royalty-Free/Corbis, f, ©Royalty-Free/Corbis j, ©Tom Stewart/Corbis, k, ©Royalty-Free/Corbis

First Indian Edition 2009

VIVA BOOKS PRIVATE LIMITED

- 4737/23 Ansari Road, Daryaganj, New Delhi 110 002
  E-mail: vivadelhi@vivagroupindia.net, Tel. 42242200
- 76, Service Industries, Shirvane, Sector 1, Nerul, Navi Mumbai 400 706
  E-mail: vivamumbai@vivagroupindia.net, Tel. 27721273, 27721274
- Jamals Fazal Chambers, 26 Greams Road, Chennai 600 006
  E-mail: vivachennai@vivagroupindia.net, Tel. 28290304, 28294241
- B-103, Jindal Towers, 21/1A/3 Darga Road, Kolkata 700 017
  E-mail: vivakolkata@vivagroupindia.net, Tel. 22836381, 22816713
- 7, Sovereign Park Apartments, 56-58, K. R. Road, Basavanagudi, Bangalore 560 004
  E-mail: vivabangalore@vivagroupindia.net, Tel. 26607409, 26607410
- 101-102 Mughal Marc Apartments, 3-4-637 to 641, Narayanguda, Hyderabad 500 029
  E-mail: vivahyderabad@vivagroupindia.net, Tel. 27564481, 27564482
- First Floor, Beevi Towers, SRM Road, Kaloor, Kochi 682 018, Kerala
  E-mail: vivakochi@vivagroupindia.net, Tel: 0484-2403055, 2403056
- H. No. 12, P. B. Road, Near Arya Hospital, Rehabari, Guwahati 781 008
  E-mail: vivaguwahati@vivagroupindia.net, Tel: 0361-2735624

www.vivagroupindia.com

Published by arrangement with
Marshall Cavendish Education
119 Wardour Street
London W1F 0OW, UK

ISBN-10: 81-309-1111-6
ISBN-13: 978-81-309-1111-3

Published by Vinod Vasishtha for Viva Books Private Limited, 4737/23, Ansari Road, Daryaganj, New Delhi - 110 002. Printed and bound by Raj Press, R-3, Inderpuri, New Delhi - 110 012.

Contents

Introduction

For the student

Just Vocabulary (Intermediate) is part of an integrated series of books designed for you to study on your own, or together with other students and a teacher. It will help you improve your knowledge and use of English words and phrases.

We have carefully chosen vocabulary areas and conversational situations in order to offer you a mix of interesting topics which will provide you with language that can be used in many different social situations.

This book has a lot of exercises that will help you to develop your vocabulary in English. It also contains plenty of pronunciation practice to help you say individual sounds and words correctly, as well as helping you to use appropriate intonation (to show if you are interested, happy, bored or sad!). In addition, there are a number of exercises to help you get used to using a dictionary.

There is an accompanying CD to help you with the many dialogues and pronunciation exercises in the book. Where you see this symbol ( ) it means that you can listen to the CD. You will also find an audioscript at the back of the book which contains all the language on the CD.

When you see this symbol ( ) it means that the answers to the practice exercises are in the answer key at the back of the book. You can check your answers there.

We are confident that this book will help you progress in English and, above all, that you will enjoy using it.

For the teacher

The *Just* series is a flexible set of teaching materials that can be used on their own, or in any combination, or as a set to form a complete integrated course. The *Just* series has been written and designed using a consistent methodological approach that allows the books to be used easily together. Each book in the series specialises in either language skills or aspects of the English language. It can be used either in class or by students working on their own.

Just Vocabulary consists of 13 units. Each unit is divided into three sections (A, B and C). The A sections teach the vocabulary for a variety of topic areas such as personal characteristics, homes, holidays, multi-word verbs, and technology and computers, as well as providing training in the effective use of dictionaries. The B sections generally focus on the language for related functional areas such as greeting and introducing people, giving opinions, and making recommendations. These sections also offer training in specific pronunciation skills. The C sections are a chance for students to consolidate what they have learnt in the unit. These sections also offer a variety of additional pronunciation activities.

All the dialogue and pronunciation material has been recorded onto the CD, and there is an audioscript near the back of the book. There is also a comprehensive answer key at the back of the book, where students can check their work.

We are confident that you will find this book a real asset and that you will also want to try the other books in the series: *Just Reading and Writing*, *Just Grammar* and *Just Listening and Speaking*.

UNIT 1

A Character description

1 **Put the missing vowels in the words to make the names of the occupations in the picture. The first one is done for you.**

a (f - - t b - l l - r) footballer

b (n - r s -) ....

c (d - s - g n - r) ....

d (p r - m - r y t - - c h - r) ....

e (- r c h - s t r - l c - n d - c t - r) ....

f (s - l d - - r) ....

g (p - r s - n - l - s s - s t - n t) ....

h (r - f - s - c - l l - c t - r) ....

i (j - - r n - l - s t) ....

j (f - r - f - g h t - r) ....

2 **Who do you think gets paid more? Put the jobs in order where 1 = the highest salary and 10 = the lowest salary. Then compare your answers with the survey results at the bottom of page 11.**

1 .... 2 .... 3 .... 4 .... 5 .... 6 .... 7 .... 8 .... 9 .... 10 ....

3 **Look at the list of adjectives. Tick the ones you know. Look up the ones you don't know in your dictionary.**

- assertive
- confident
- considerate
- decisive
- emotional
- enthusiastic
- friendly
- happy
- honest
- hospitable
- intelligent
- interesting
- kind
- loyal
- patient
- pleasant
- romantic
- sensitive
- sincere
- sympathetic

4 **Which three of the qualities listed in Exercise 3 would you expect in each of the people in Exercise 1?**

a A footballer should be assertive, confident and decisive.

b ....

c ....

d ....

e ....

f ....

g ....

h ....

i ....

j ....

Using a dictionary: definitions and examples

5 Look at the entries for *assertive* and *sensitive*, and answer the following questions.

claim that something is true
assertive /ə'sɜːtɪv/ adj behaving in a confident way in which you are quick to express your opinions and feelings: *You need to be more assertive to succeed in business.* —**assertively** adv, **assertiveness** noun [U]

sensitive /'sensətɪv/ adj ★★★
3 showing that you care about someone or something and do not want to cause offence: *This is a difficult case which needs sensitive and skilful handling.* ♦ **+to** *The police should be more sensitive to the needs of local communities.*

a Which are the definitions?

assertive: ....

sensitive: ....

b Which are the examples? ....

6 We give words opposite meanings by adding a prefix like *un-*, *in-*, *im-*, *dis-*.

For example: *necessary* → *unnecessary* *appear* → *disappear*

Give the opposite meaning for each word from Exercise 3 by choosing the correct prefix.

un- unassertive, ... im- ....

in- inconsiderate, ... dis- ....

7 Using some of the words in the box below or their opposites (for example, *indecisive*), complete the sentences. The first one is done for you.

decisive
enthusiastic
friendly
honest
hospitable
kind
loyal
patient
romantic
sensitive
sincere
sympathetic

a Steve can never make decisions. He is very indecisive .

b You can believe what they say. The staff seem very ....

c You never feel welcome in Lisa's house. She's very ....

d Your son is very .... He's always telling lies.

e .... people are kind, listen to your troubles, and try to help.

f Andrew gets very .... if he has to wait too long for anything.

g In fairy stories stepmothers are often very .... to their stepdaughters, though no one really knows why.

h Don't expect Derek to cry when he sees moving films. He's a very .... person!

i Amna's always keen on things – she always likes to get involved. She's a very .... person.

j It is easy to offend John because he's a very .... man.

k Yumi will always defend you when other people are attacking you. She's very ....

B Meeting people

1 Before you listen to Track 1, read the dialogue and complete it with the following lines.

Not much really.
Oh, all right.
Oh, I mean I only started last week. It's my first job. What about you?
That sounds interesting.
Yeah, nice to meet you too.

JANE: Come on, Polly, there's someone I'd like you to meet.

POLLY: (a) ……………………

JANE: Andy, this is Polly. She's in advertising too.

ANDY: Oh, hi. Nice to meet you.

POLLY: (b) ……………………

ANDY: What do you do in advertising?

POLLY: (c) ……………………

ANDY: Sorry?

POLLY: (d) ……………………

ANDY: Me? Oh well, I'm working on a TV commercial for an Internet bank at the moment.

POLLY: (e) ……………………

ANDY: Yes, yes it is.

Now listen to Track 1. Were you right?

2 In each box, match the words in the two columns to make statements or questions. The first one is done for you.

a There's someone b Andy, this c I'd like you d Polly's e Nice to	in advertising. I'd like you to meet. meet you. is Polly. to meet Andy.
f Are you g Do you like h How do you i What are you working on j What do	you do? at the moment? know our host? what you do? a friend of Polly's?
k Oh l That m What a	coincidence! I'm an actor too. really? sounds interesting.

a There's someone I'd like you to meet.
b ……………………
c ……………………
d ……………………
e ……………………
f ……………………
g ……………………
h ……………………
i ……………………
j ……………………
k ……………………
l ……………………
m ……………………

3 **Put the words and punctuation in the correct order to make sentences. Write them in the correct place in the conversation.**

- a / coincidence / . / That's
- teacher / be / you / a / ? /young / bit / Aren't / to / a
- a / ask / Can / ? / I / question / you
- ? / Do / enjoy / studying / you / zoology
- him / I / like / . / think / you'll
- a / I'm / . / teacher
- , / . / meet / nice / to / too / Yeah / you
- someone / I'd / like / meet / . / to / There's / you

SUSAN: Come with me, Ruth. (a) ....

RUTH: Oh, that sounds interesting.

SUSAN: Yes, well (b) .... Mark, this is Ruth.

MARK: Nice to meet you Ruth.

RUTH: (c) ....

MARK: What do you do?

RUTH: I'm a zoology student.

MARK: Oh really. (d) ....

RUTH: I don't really know. I've only just got here. My course hasn't started. But what about you? What do you do?

MARK: (e) ....

RUTH: Oh really. What do you teach?

MARK: Zoology.

RUTH: (f) ....

MARK: Yes, I suppose it is.

RUTH: (g) ....

MARK: Of course.

RUTH: (h) ....

MARK: Yes, I suppose I am. But like you, I've only just started.

Pronunciation: hearing sounds

4 **Say these words:**

small always organised four sort more

What sound do all the words share, /æ/ like *cat*, /ɔː/ like *call*, or /ʌ/ like *bus*? ....

5 **List which of the following words share the same sound as the words above.**

all	seem	ought	store
arm	smell	walk	out
door	stare	work	saw

Now listen to Track 2 on the tape. Were you correct?

C Check out

Word list

assertive confident conscientious considerate decisive designer doctor emotional enthusiastic firefighter footballer friendly happy honest hospitable impatient intelligent interesting journalist kind loyal nurse occupation orchestral conductor organised patient personal assistant (PA) pleasant primary teacher refuse collector romantic salary sensitive sincere soldier sympathetic

1 Which are your five favourite words from the word list here?

a ....

b ....

c ....

d ....

e ....

2 Write words from the word list for these two meaning groups.

a Occupations: ....

....

b Characteristics: ....

....

Pronunciation

3 a Complete the table with the three- and four-syllable words from the word list. Where is the stress in each case?

three syllables	four syllables
assertive	considerate

Listen to Track 3 and check your answers.

b How many different ways is the letter 'c' pronounced in the words in the word list? ....

Listen to Track 4 and check your answer.

4 Read the questions and listen to Track 5. Does the speaker's voice go *up* or *down* at the end of the question in each case? Circle the correct word.

a What do you think of Lisa? up / down

b What do you do in advertising? up / down

c Have you two met before? up / down

d How long have you known Ruth? up / down

e Can I ask you a question? up / down

f Do you enjoy studying zoology? up / down

g What time is your taxi coming? up / down

Say the questions in the same way as the speakers on Track 5.

Survey results

In 2003 Opinion Surveys UK (OS UK™) conducted a survey in Great Britain.
They asked people the following two questions.

1 Who do you think gets paid most? Who you think gets paid least?
2 Who do you think should get paid most? Who do you think should get paid least?

The results are shown in the following table.

	Question 1	Question 2
designer	4	5
firefighter	8	2
footballer	1	1
journalist	3	6
nurse	6	3
orchestral conductor	2	8
personal assistant	5	7
primary teacher	7	4
refuse collector	10	9
soldier	9	10

UNIT 2

A Stronger adjectives

1 **We sometimes want to use stronger adjectives when describing things.**

A: I was late for work again this morning.
B: Was your boss angry?
A: Angry? She was furious!

Match the following adjectives with the adjectives in the table. The first one is done for you.

- big
- dirty
- fantastic
- fascinating
- freezing
- funny
- furious
- hot
- surprising
- terrible
- terrifying

Ordinary adjectives	Stronger adjectives
angry	furious
bad	
	enormous
cold	
	filthy
frightening	
	hilarious
good	
	boiling
interesting	
	amazing

2 **Listen to Track 6. What are the missing words?**

3 Look at how we can use adverbs before adjectives, and then do the exercise below.

ADVERB + ADJECTIVE

We can use *adverbs* (e.g. *fairly, really*) to make the meaning of an *adjective* stronger or weaker:

It's fairly cold. *It's really cold.*

less than *very*	*very*	more than *very*
fairly quite rather pretty	really	absolutely completely

But note:
- we usually only use ***absolutely*** or ***completely*** with stronger adjectives; for example, we don't say *absolutely nice*, but we do say *absolutely lovely*
- we don't use ***very*** with stronger adjectives because these adjectives already mean '*very*' (for example, *furious* means *very angry*)
- ***pretty*** is much more common in informal speech than in writing.

Put a cross [*X*] by the four adverb + adjective combinations that are not possible.

a pretty amazing [ ]
b absolutely big [ ]
c really terrifying [ ]
d very interesting [ ]
e absolutely fascinating [ ]
f very boiling [ ]
g rather funny [ ]
h completely interesting [ ]
i very enormous [ ]
j quite fascinating [ ]

Using a dictionary: word grammar

4 Look at the following dictionary entries for *absolute* and *absolutely*, and answer the questions that follow.

absolute /'æbsəlu:t/ *adj* **[always before noun]** **1** complete *absolute power/control* • *The party was an absolute disaster.* **2** definite *There was no absolute proof of fraud.*

absolutely /ˌæbsə'lu:tli/ *adv* **1** completely *The food was absolutely delicious.* • *She absolutely hated the place.* • *There's absolutely nothing (= nothing at all) left.* **2 Absolutely.** used to strongly agree with someone *"Do you think it helped his career?" "Absolutely."* **3 Absolutely not.** used to strongly disagree with someone or to agree with something negative *"Are you suggesting that we should just ignore the problem?" "No, absolutely not."*

a What part of speech (adjective, adverb, noun, preposition, verb etc.) is each word?

absolute: ....

absolutely: ....

b What kind of word follows each word?

absolute: ....

absolutely: (1) ....

(2) ....

c When do we use *absolutely not*, in speech or in writing?

....

5 Using the adjectives from Exercise 1 and adverbs from Exercise 4, complete the following exchanges. One is done for you.

a – Look at my new picture.
– Wow! It's absolutely enormous!

b – What did your father say when you told him?
– He was ....

c – Did you enjoy the meal he cooked for us?
– No, it was ....

d – What do you think of the new CD?
– It's ....

e – Why are you looking at me like that?
– You're ....

f – Where are you going?
– To have a swim. I'm ....

g – Did you enjoy the movie?
– It was ....

h – Are you warm enough in your tent?
– No, I'm ....

B Giving opinions

1 Listen to Track 7 and complete the conversation.

A: Have you ever seen the original film of *Psycho*?

B: Yes.

A: ....

B: It was absolutely terrifying.

C: (Do) you really think so?

B: ....

C: No, not really. It's not my kind of film. I thought it was rather boring.

2 What phrase do the speakers use to:

a ... ask if something has happened? ....

b ... ask for opinions? ....

c ... give an opinion? ....

3 Is the following language used to agree or disagree with opinions? Put A (*agree*) or D (*disagree*) in the brackets. The first one is done for you.

a Do you really think so? [D]

b I completely agree. [ ]

c Yes it was, wasn't it? [ ]

d I don't agree at all. [ ]

e I don't think so. [ ]

f You're absolutely right. [ ]

g Yes. I thought so, too. [ ]

4 Complete the conversation with one word for each gap.

BRIAN: Did you see *The Sixth Sense* on (a) .... last night?

DAVE: No. But I (b) .... it when it first came out some years (c) ....

BRIAN: Oh well, I'd never seen it (d) .... so I was looking forward to it.

DAVE: What did you (e) .... of it?

BRIAN: It was absolutely terrifying.

DAVE: (f) .... you really think so?

BRIAN: Why? Don't you (g) .... with me?

DAVE: No, not really. I (h) .... it was rather boring when I saw it, I remember.

BRIAN: (i) .... ? You can't be serious.

DAVE: Why not? I mean I (j) .... what the ending was going to be (k) .... the first five minutes.

BRIAN: Did you? I (l) .... I never guessed.

DAVE: Oh well. But I (m) .... the little boy was good.

BRIAN: Yes, I thought so (**n**) .... He was completely believable.

FELICITY: Hi you (**o**) .... What are you talking about?

BRIAN: That (**p**) ...., *The Sixth Sense*. It was on the box (**q**) .... night.

FELICITY: Oh yes. I videoed it. I'm (**r**) .... to watch it later. Will I enjoy it?

DAVE: (**s**) .... not. It's not a great (**t**) .... , frankly.

BRIAN: Don't listen to him. It is a (**u**) .... film. Really frightening.

DAVE: I don't (**v**) .... at all. I mean you guess almost (**w**) .... that the main character, the Bruce Willis, character, (**x**) .... a ...

BRIAN: Don't tell her the ending Dave, you (**y**) .... ruin it for her. That's not fair.

DAVE: You're (**z**) .... right. Sorry.

Pronunciation: spelling and sounds

5 Listen to Track 8 to hear the different pronunciations of the letter 'a'. Put the blue words into the correct columns. Some will go in two columns. One has been done for you.

I like playing games in my head.
Absolutely fascinating.
The film was amazing.
It was rather boring when I saw it, I remember.
I went to all his films when I was at school.
What happened at the end of the film?
I completely agree.
It makes me very angry!
Call me when you've seen the film.
Have you seen any films recently?
I haven't read that book.

a /æ/ *cat*, *hat*	b /ɔː/ *four*, *more*	c /ə/ *a bottle of milk*	d /e/ *many*, *said*	e /eɪ/ *pay*, *today*
				playing

6 Can you add any more words to the columns? Can you find any other ways to pronounce the letter 'a'?

....

....

....

....

C Check out

1 **Which words and phrases in the word list do you already know? Circle any 'new' words and look them up in a dictionary.**

Word list

absolutely amazing angry bad big boiling cold dirty enormous fairly fantastic fascinating filthy freezing frightening funny furious good hilarious hot interesting pretty (adv.) quite rather really surprising terrible terrifying very

Pronunciation: spelling and sounds

2 **Complete the following tasks.**

a List the words from the word list that you find easy to pronounce.

....

....

....

....

b Now list words from the word list that you find the most difficult to pronounce. Look at a dictionary to see how they should be said and practise saying them.

....

....

....

....

c Find all the words in the word list with the letter 'a'. How many different ways is it pronounced?

....

....

....

....

Listen to Track 9 and check the pronunciation of the words in 2c.

3 **Circle the stressed syllables in the adjectives and their *intensifiers* (words that make them stronger or weaker). Put a line under the strongest syllable. The first one is done for you.**

a He's rather interesting.
b I was pretty scared.
c It was absolutely amazing.
d It was absolutely hilarious.
e She was rather angry.
f They're really good.
g Your room's absolutely filthy!

Listen to Track 10 and repeat the sentences.

UNIT 3

A Shopping

Using a dictionary: noun types

1 Look at the dictionary entry for *shopping* and answer the questions which follow.

shop·ping S2 W3 /ˈʃɒpɪŋ $ ʃɑː-/ *n* [U]
1 the activity of going to shops and buying things: *Late-night shopping is becoming very popular.* | **shopping expedition/trip** *She's gone on a **shopping trip** to New York.* | *I **went on a shopping spree*** (=went shopping and bought a lot of things) *at the weekend and spent far too much money.* | *I've got to do some last-minute shopping.* | *the busy Christmas shopping season* → WINDOW-SHOPPING
2 do the shopping to go shopping

a Is *shopping* countable or uncountable? ....

b How do you know? ....

c What does $ mean here? ....

2 The words in the box can be used together with *shopping*. Can you put them in the right place in the table? The first one is done for you.

trolley	the	last-minute	malls
centre	expedition	late-night	serious
complex	go	bag	Sunday
do	Internet	list	window-

a *shopping* + noun (to create a new compound noun)	b adjective / noun / verb } + *shopping*
shopping trolley	

3 Use the *shopping* phrases from Exercise 2 to complete what you think these people are saying.

a I've still got some .... to do before the party tomorrow.

b I don't really need to buy anything. I'm just .... to see what the new fashions are like.

c I prefer to do all my shopping at a .... because everything you need is there, and there's usually somewhere to have a coffee when you've finished.

d How do you fancy a really good ....? We could stay in town for the whole day.

e I don't agree with .... We should have one day when everyone can relax.

f Excuse me sir, where did you get this ....?

Now listen to Track 11. Were you correct?

4 Complete the questionnaire with shopping phrases from Exercise 2, and then circle the answer you would give. Follow the first example.

SHOPPING QUESTIONNAIRE	
a Do you ever go on a major *shopping expedition* which lasts the whole day?	always / usually / often / sometimes / never
b Do you ever forget things and have to rush and do ....?	always / usually / often / sometimes / never
c Is it possible to do .... where you live or do all the shops close early?	always / usually / often / sometimes / never
d Do you ever spend time .... without actually buying anything?	always / usually / often / sometimes / never
e Do you ever go .... at the end of a long day at work?	always / usually / often / sometimes / never
f Do you use a .... when you go to the supermarket?	always / usually / often / sometimes / never
g Do you ever .... for everyone in the house?	always / usually / often / sometimes / never
h Do you ever use your computer to do ....?	always / usually / often / sometimes / never

B Asking for help in a shop

1 Before you listen to Track 12, put the following lines (1–4) in the right places in the conversations below.

1 Do you know where I could find some?
2 They might be able to help.
3 They're over there by those shirts.
4 Let me know if I can help you with anything.

GARY: Can I help you?
KYLIE: No thanks. I'm just looking around.
GARY: OK.
(a) ....
....
....
KYLIE: Thanks.
GARY: No problem.

ANDY: Excuse me.
GARY: Yes. How can I help you?
ANDY: I'm looking for Takez jeans.
GARY: I'm afraid we don't sell Takez.
ANDY: Oh, that's a pity.
(b) ....
....
....
GARY: Well, you could try the shop on the corner.
(c) ....
....
....
ANDY: Thanks.
GARY: You're welcome.

POLLY: Excuse me. Do you have any belts?
GARY: Yes we do.
(d) ....
....
....
POLLY: Oh yes, so they are. Thanks.

Now listen to Track 12. Were you correct?

2 Look at the following list of clothes. Tick the words you know.

belt	[ ]	skirt	[ ]	cap	[ ]
dress	[ ]	socks	[ ]	fleece	[ ]
gloves	[ ]	sweater	[ ]	sandals	[ ]
hat	[ ]	(a pair of) trousers	[ ]	shorts	[ ]
jeans	[ ]	T-shirt	[ ]	(a pair of) tights	[ ]
shirt	[ ]				

Find out the meaning of the words you didn't tick by using a dictionary.

Pronunciation: same sound

3 Find words which share a vowel sound on their stressed syllable. Join them together. One is done for you.

Listen to Track 13 to check your answers.

anything belt

cap dress every fleece gloves

hat help jeans many much several

shirt skirt some sweater T-shirt

welcome please

4 Who's wearing what? Write a list for each person. The first one is done for you.

a Barbara: a dress, a sweater, boots and a hat.

b Charlene: ....

c Donald: ....

d Phoebe: ....

e Margaret: ....

f Ashley: ....

Barbara Charlene Donald Phoebe Margaret Ashley

5 Put the following lines in the correct place in the conversation.

1 Umm actually, perhaps you can help me. I'm looking for a fleece.
2 No thanks, I'm just looking around.
3 Oh right. Thanks.
4 Oh, umm, excuse me, just before I go and look at the fleeces, do you have any of those Arguski belts – you know the brown and red ones?
5 Thanks.
6 Thanks. Good idea. I'll go there now.
7 That's a pity. Do you know where I could buy one of those belts?
8 They'll sell them in the department store opposite, won't they?

A: Can I help you?
B: (a) ....
A: OK. Let me know if I can help you with anything.
B: (b) ....
A: No problem.
B: (c) ....
A: Oh right. The fleeces are over there by the jeans.
B: (d) ....
A: You're welcome.
B: (e) ....
A: No, I'm sorry. We don't sell Arguski designs.
B: (f) ....
A: You could try the department store opposite. They might be able to help.
B: (g) ....
A: But what about the fleeces?
B: (h) ....
A: Yes. I suppose they will.

C Check out

Word list

belt cap fleece gloves hat jeans last-minute shopping late-night shopping sandals serious shopping shirt shopping bag shopping centre shopping complex shopping list shopping mall shopping spree shopping trolley shorts skirt socks Sunday shopping sweater (a pair of) tights to do the shopping to go shopping (a pair of) trousers T-shirt window-shopping

1 Group the words in the word list into different meaning groups (such as 'clothing', 'places' etc). How many meaning groups are there?

....

....

....

....

....

....

....

....

....

....

....

....

....

....

....

....

Pronunciation: same vowel sounds

2 a Write down pairs of words from the word list with the same vowel sound (e.g. *cap/hat*).

....
....
....
....

Listen to Track 14 and check.

b Which words in the list have the same sound / ʃ / as *shopping*?

....

Listen to Track 15 and check.

3 Listen to the pairs of sentences on Track 16. Are they the *Same* or *Different*? Write S or D in the brackets.

a [ ] d [ ]
b [ ] e [ ]
c [ ] f [ ]

Listen again and repeat the sentences.

UNIT 4

A Holidays

1 **Match the statements with the people in the pictures. Put the number in the brackets.**

a 'I like going to museums and galleries – at my age sightseeing is my favourite activity.' [ ]
b 'I like somewhere off the beaten track – you know, places that aren't full of tourists.' [ ]
c 'I love pony-trekking over the hills.' [ ]
d 'We enjoy swimming and sunbathing – and all the other activities on board like the casino and the nightclub.' [ ]
e 'We like holidays that our children enjoy as well. That's why we go camping.' [ ]
f 'When I'm on holiday I go clubbing most nights.' [ ]

2 **Use a dictionary to check the meaning of any words in the box that you do not know, then put the words and expressions in the appropriate rows. Some words may go in more than one row.**

backpacking	nightlife
museums	sunbathing
boating	(swimming) pool
campsite	resort
galleries	clubbing
culture	surfing
excellent facilities	tourist
excursion	vacation
pony-trekking	waterski
hotel	swimming
luxury	

a an adventure or outdoor holiday	
b a camping holiday	
c a cruise	
d a package holiday	
e a sightseeing holiday	

Using a dictionary: varieties of English

3 Look at the dictionary entries for *holiday*, *holidaymaker* and *vacation*. Answer the questions that follow.

hol·i·day[1] S2 W2 /ˈhɒlədi, -deɪ $ ˈhɑːlədeɪ/ *n*
1 [C,U] *BrE* also **holidays** a time of rest from work, school etc; ⊟ **vacation** *AmE*: *The school holidays start tomorrow.* | **on holiday** *I'm away on holiday until the 1st of June.* | *Won't your business suffer if you **take a holiday**?*

holiday[2] *v* [I] *BrE* to spend your holiday in a place – used especially in news reports; ⊟ **vacation** *AmE*: [+in/at] *They're holidaying in Majorca.*

hol·i·day·mak·er /ˈhɒlədi,meɪkə $ ˈhɑːlədeɪ,meɪkər/ *n* [C] *BrE* someone who has travelled to a place on holiday; → **tourist**; ⊟ **vacationer** *AmE*

va·ca·tion[1] S2 W3 /vəˈkeɪʃən $ veɪ-/ *n*
1 [C,U] *especially AmE* a holiday, or time spent not working

vacation[2] *v* [I] *AmE* to go somewhere for a holiday: [+in/at] *The Bernsteins are vacationing in Europe.*

a Which words can be both a noun and a verb in:

... American English? ....

... British English? ....

How do you know? ....

b In American English, which word can be used for the time when students are not studying?

How do you know? ....

c Which speakers use the word *holidaymaker*? Which speakers use the word *vacationer*?

How do you know? ....

d Using your own dictionary, find at least two more examples where American and British English have different words for the same thing. ....

4 Complete the sentences with one word for each gap.

a A holiday on a large ship is called a ....

b I think activity holidays are really .... They're certainly not boring.

c If you want to see things from many years ago you can visit a ....

d People who spend too much time .... often get burnt.

e People who go on holiday to see different places are called ....

f Rooms that are .... - .... are always cooler than those that are not.

g When you go on a holiday in which everything has been arranged for you, this is called a ....

5 Take the first letter of each answer from Exercise 4. Rearrange the letters to find where Henry is staying.

'We always stay on a _ _ _ _ _ _ _ _ e.'

6 Put the letters in order to make holiday and tourism words.

a (a a b d o r) ....

b (a a b c c g i k k n p) ....

c (c e i n o r s u x) ....

d (a e g l l r y) ....

e (a a d e h i k l m o r y) ....

f (e o r r s t) ....

g (e e g g h i i n s s t) ....

h (a a c i n o t v) ....

7 What is your favourite kind of holiday? What is your least favourite kind of holiday? Write a paragraph for each.

a My favourite kind of holiday is ....

....

because ....

....

b My least favourite kind of holiday is ....

....

because ....

....

B Recommending holidays

1 Before you listen to Track 17, put the travel agent's questions and recommendations, in the box, into the correct gaps to complete the conversation.

TRAVEL AGENT: (a) ....

BEN: We'd like to book a holiday.

DUNCAN: Yes, can you recommend anything?

TRAVEL AGENT: (b) ....

DUNCAN: Oh you know, sun, sea, sand, the usual.

TRAVEL AGENT: (c) ....

BEN: Well, we've been to Spain once already.

TRAVEL AGENT: (d) ....

DUNCAN: Italy? That's a great idea, but actually we'd prefer somewhere a bit more, well, exotic.

TRAVEL AGENT: (e) ....

BEN: I don't think we could afford that.

TRAVEL AGENT: (f) ....

DUNCAN: Yes, but is it worth it?

TRAVEL AGENT: (g) ....

BEN: Can I have a look at the brochure?

TRAVEL AGENT: (h) ....

BEN: Thanks.

- ❍ Actually, it's probably not as expensive as you think.
- ❍ All right then, can I suggest Rio de Janeiro?
- ❍ OK, what about somewhere in Spain, say Sitges near Barcelona?
- ❍ Sure. Take your time.
- ❍ Well, it's definitely worth considering.
- ❍ Well, what kind of holiday do you want?
- ❍ Well then, how about Sorrento in Italy?
- ❍ Yes, can I help you?

Now listen to Track 17. Were you correct?

2 Look at how we can ask for and give recommendations.

ASKING FOR AND GIVING RECOMMENDATIONS

1 We can ask for recommendations like this:
Can you recommend somewhere to stay near the sea?
Can you suggest a good place for a holiday?
Have you got any ideas about a good hotel?
Is it worth { visiting Wellington? / seeing Auckland? }
Is Paris worth { a visit? / considering? }

2 We can make recommendations like this:
What about (going to) Alaska?
How about the Hotel Stella?
Have you thought of (going to) London?
Why don't you try somewhere in Portugal?
If it was me, I'd go somewhere cheaper.
Why don't you give it a try?

3 We can reply to recommendations like this:
That sounds like a great idea!
That's exactly what I was looking for.
That's not quite what { I was looking for. / I was thinking of. }
That's a great idea, but I'd rather go somewhere more comfortable.
I think we'd prefer something a bit less expensive.

Make new questions and sentences by replacing the blue words with words of your own.

Here are some examples:
Can you recommend somewhere with really good sports facilities?
If it was me, I'd go somewhere more beautiful.

....

....

....

....

....

....

....

....

....

....

....

....

....

....

....

....

....

Pronunciation: pitch and intonation

3 Listen to people accepting recommendations on Track 18. Are they enthusiastic or unenthusiastic?

a That sounds fantastic. ....

b That sounds like a great idea. ....

c That's exactly what I want. ....

d That's just right. ....

e That's incredible. ....

f That's a great suggestion. ....

4 Say the sentences using the same pitch and intonation as the speakers.

C Check out

Word list

adventure holiday backpacking boating camping campsite clubbing cruise culture excellent facilities excursion gallery holiday holidaymaker hotel luxury museum nightlife off the beaten track package holiday pony-trekking pool resort sightseeing sunbathe surfing swimming tourist touristy trekking vacation waterski

1 Imagine you are going to be stranded on a desert island and you can only take five words from the word list with you. Which ones will you take and why? Here is an example:

I'll take pony-trekking because I like the sound of it – and I could get around the island more easily.

Pronunciation

2 **a** How many words can you find in the word list that have the sound /æ/ – like *cat*?

Listen to Track 19 and check.

b Find the one odd word in the following lists.

Think about sounds.

1 package, vacation, backpacking, camping, fantastic
2 clubbing, cruise, public, sunbathe, fun

Think about syllables.

3 backpacking, boating, excursion, holiday, waterski
4 camping, culture, hotel, museum, sunbathe

Think about stress.

5 gallery, nightlife, sunbathe, resort, swimming
6 holiday, gallery, excursion, sightseeing, luxury

Listen to Track 20 and check.

3 Listen to Track 21. Circle the word you hear.

a	big	pig	c	cheap	sheep	e	good	wood	g	better	wetter	i	cruise	choose
b	hot	hat	d	nice	noise	f	fat	foot	h	plane	plan	j	sight	seat

Listen again and repeat the words.

A Homes and houses

1 Look at these words and find pairs of words with opposite meanings.

bare	untidy
cold	spacious
cramped	tidy
cluttered	dark
light	warm

....

....

....

....

2 Choose one of the following homes.

Using words from Exercise 1 and any other words you know, list the advantages and disadvantages of the home you have chosen in the table below.

Here is an example:

Your choice: ......tent...... Advantages: light, easy to carry	Disadvantages: uncomfortable, cold
Your choice: .... Advantages:	Disadvantages:

3 Make new words by adding *home* to the following words. Use the new words in the newspaper headlines below. The first one is done for you.

___sick ___coming ___less ___-grown ___work ___-made

a ..Home-grown.. lettuce sells best

b .... man wins lottery, buys house

c .... cake poisons entire village

d .... couple return after only 72 hours away

e .... crisis in our schools

f .... celebration cancelled when returning son misses transatlantic flight

4 Write the words in the box beside the right numbers below. The first one has been done for you.

basement	garage
block of flats	garden
bungalow	gate
cottage	ground floor
fence	terraced house
flat	studio flat
first floor	
semi-detached house	

1 ....block of flats........
2 ....
3 ....
4 ....
5 ....
6 ....
7 ....
8 ....
9 ....
10 ....
11 ....
12 ....
13 ....
14 ....

Using a dictionary: reading the whole entry

5 Look at the dictionary entry for *garden* and answer the following questions.

gar·den[1] S1 W1 /ˈɡɑːdn $ ˈɡɑːr-/ *n*
1 [C] *BrE* the area of land next to a house, where there are flowers, grass, and other plants, and often a place for people to sit; **yard** *AmE*: *He's outside in the garden.* | *Grace brought us some flowers from her garden.* | *Our house has a small garden.* | *a garden **shed*** | **back/front garden** (=at the back or the front of the house)
2 [C] *AmE* a part of the area next to a house, which has plants and flowers in it: **vegetable/herb/rose garden** *The house has a beautiful herb garden.*
3 gardens [plural] a large area of land where plants and flowers are grown so that the public can go and see them: *the **Botanical Gardens** at Kew*
4 Gardens *BrE* used in the name of streets: *211 Roland Gardens* → KITCHEN GARDEN, MARKET GARDEN; → **lead sb up the garden path** at LEAD[1] (12)

a Is *garden* an adjective, adverb, noun, preposition or verb? How do you know?
....

b How is it pronounced? ....
....

c What equivalent word is there in American English? ....

d How many different meanings are given?
....

B Welcoming people

1 Look at the picture. What are they saying to each other?

....

....

Listen to Track 22. Were you correct?

2 Match the phrases in the two columns to complete the welcoming sentences. The first one is done for you.

Can I get you	finding us?
Can I take	into the sitting room.
Did you have any trouble	something to drink?
Do you want/need	to see you!
Go on	to wash your hands/freshen up?
How nice	for coming.
Thanks	your coat?

a Can I get you something to drink?

b Can I take ....

c Did ....

d Do ....

e Go ....

f How ....

g Thanks ....

Listen to Track 23 and repeat the phrases.

3 Put the phrases from Exercise 2 in the correct gaps.

a 'Can I get you something to drink?' 'Yes please. I'd like an orange juice.'

b '..........' 'No. It was quite straightforward, actually.'

c '..........' 'Thank you.'

d '..........' 'Thank you. Is it through here?'

e '..........' 'Yes, that would be nice. Where's the bathroom?'

f '..........' 'Well, thanks for inviting us.'

g '..........' 'Yes. It's great to be here.'

Pronunciation: stress in phrases

4 **Look at the phrases in Exercise 3. Listen to Track 24 and write a line under the word or the part of the word where the speakers place the main stress.**

I'd like an orange juice.

5 **Repeat the phrases after the speakers on Track 24.**

6 **Rearrange the words and punctuation to make appropriate sentences and questions.**

a coming / . / for / Thanks

Thanks for coming.

b I / get / drink / ? / you / something / Can / to

c trouble / ? / you / here / any / finding / have / your / Did / way

d ? / take / coat / Can / your / I

e Do / ? / up / to / need / you / freshen

f you / . / nice / to / How / see

g bad / . / , / lost / bit / got / a / but / too / it / wasn't / We

h ? / Yes / . / you / Have / an / got / orange / juice / please

i ? / bathroom / Can / is / me / tell / the / where / you

j great / you / to / . / It's / see

k , / I'll / if / it / all / I / on / No / right / . / think / keep / that's /.

7 **Match the sentences and questions from Exercise 6 with these replies. The first one is done for you.**

a 'Can I get you something to drink?'
'Yes, please. I'd love an apple juice, if you've got one.'

b '...'
'Yes, please. It's quite warm in here.'

c '...'
'No. Your directions were absolutely perfect.'

d '...'
'Yes please. I'd like to wash my hands.'

e '...'
'It's nice to see you too.'

f '...'
'Great to see you too.'

g '...'
'Why? It's not cold in here.'

h '...'
'Well, at least you're here now.'

i '...'
'No, I'm afraid not. But we've got mango juice or apple juice.'

j '...'
'It's just along the corridor. Last door on the right.'

C Check out

Word list

accident accidental bare basement block of flats bungalow campsite camper van cluttered cold cottage cramped dark fence first floor flat garage garden gate ground floor homecoming homeless home-made homesick homework houseboat light mobile home semi-detached house spacious studio flat tent terraced house tidy untidy warm

1 Think about which six words in the word list will be most useful to you in the future. Why?

....

....

....

2 Write some of the words from the word list in the appropriate box here.

Words with a positive feeling

Words with a negative feeling

Pronunciation: same sounds

3 **a** What sound do all these words have in common?

bungalow	homeless
cold	mobile home
cope	studio
go	

....

Listen to Track 25 and check.

b Can you find other words in the word list, on page 34 which include the same sound?

....

Listen to Track 26 and check.

c Which words in the word list start with the following sounds:

/bl/: ....

/kr/: ....

/gr/: ....

/sp/: ....

Listen to Track 27 and check.

d Which sound do you find the most difficult to say?

e List some other words that start with these sounds:

/bl/: ....

/kr/: ....

/gr/: ....

/sp/: ....

4 Listen to the phrases on Track 28 and circle the two stressed syllables in these sentences. Put a line under the syllable with the biggest stress.

- **a** It's great to see you.
- **b** Oh, this is great!
- **c** Can I take your coat?
- **d** It's a bit cramped in here.
- **e** I've just won a prize.
- **f** Can I get you something to drink?
- **g** Thanks for inviting us.

Listen to Track 28 again and repeat the phrases.

UNIT 6

A History and biography

1 Complete the sentences in each box using the words in the column on the left.

IN A COURT OF LAW

guilty
prison
sentence
accuse

a I .... you of stealing £250,000.

b We think he is ....

c I .... you to ten years in ....

HIGH ADVENTURE

disguised
escaped
pirate
soldiers
captured

d Mad John, the ...., was .... by the King's ....

e They put him in prison, but he .... , ... as a woman.

WAR AND PEACE

defeated
crowned
elected
conquered

f When he .... the country, he .... himself king.

g Ten years later the king was .... in battle.

h The people .... a president instead.

MURDER

died
executed
poison
shot
stabbed

i The first Lord Mountebank .... when he drank ....

j Ten years later someone .... his son with a knife.

k The third Lord Mountebank was ....

l The fourth was .... by a jealous lover.

FAMILY MATTERS

born
brought up
divorced
educated
inherited
married

m She was .... in 1923. She was .... by her uncle.

n She was .... at the best school in America.

o She .... $35 million when her uncle died.

p She .... three times – and got .... three times too.

2 Complete the table with the related past participle and noun for each verb. The first one is done for you.

a Verb (infinitive)	b Verb (past participle)	c Noun
accuse	accused	accusation
conquer		
crown		
defeat		
die		
disguise		
divorce		
educate		
elect		
escape		
execute		
imprison		
inherit		
marry		
poison		
sentence		
shoot		
stab		

Using a dictionary: same word, different meanings

3 Look at the dictionary entry for *crown*.

a How many different meanings are given for the noun? ....

b If 'S3' means that *crown* is one of the 3000 most common words in spoken English, what does 'W3' mean? ....

....

....

c What does '[C]' mean? Is that the same as 'usually singular'?

....

....

....

crown[1] S3 W3 /kraʊn/ *n*
1 HAT FOR KING/QUEEN [C] **a)** a circle made of gold and decorated with jewels, worn by kings and queens on their heads **b)** a circle, sometimes made of things such as leaves or flowers, worn by someone who has won a special honour
2 COUNTRY'S RULER the crown a) the position of being king or queen: *The treaty of Troyes made Henry V heir to the crown of France.* **b)** the government of a country such as Britain that is officially led by a king or queen: *He has retired from the service of the Crown.*
3 TOOTH [C] an artificial top for a damaged tooth
4 HEAD [usually singular] the top part of a hat or someone's head: [+of] *auburn hair piled high on the crown of her head* | *a hat with a high crown*
5 HILL [usually singular] the top of a hill or something shaped like a hill: [+of] *They drove to the crown of Zion hill and on into town.* | *The masonry at the crown of the arch is paler than on either curve.*
6 SPORTS [usually singular] the position you have if you have won an important sports competition: *Can she retain her Wimbledon crown?* | *He went on to win the world crown in 2001.*
7 MONEY [C] **a)** the standard unit of money in some European countries: *Swedish crowns* **b)** an old British coin. Four crowns made a pound.
8 PICTURE [C] a mark, sign, BADGE etc in the shape of a crown, used especially to show rank or quality

C

B Paying compliments

1 **Before you listen to Track 29, put these lines in the correct conversations.**

I was given them by my aunt.
From that shop opposite the bank.
It was a present from my girlfriend.

HELEN: That's a really nice jacket.
SAM: Oh, thanks.
HELEN: Where did you get it?
SAM: (a) ....
HELEN: Oh yes. I know the one. Well, it really suits you.
SAM: Thanks.

JASON: I like your shirt.
LEO: Do you?
JASON: Yes.
LEO: (b) ....
JASON: Well, it looks good on you. What's it made of?
LEO: I don't know. Cotton, I think.

SUNITA: Those are really nice earrings.
KAREN: I'm glad you like them.
SUNITA: Where did you get them?
KAREN: (c) .... They're from Japan, I think.
SUNITA: Well, I think they're great.

Now listen to Track 29. Were you correct?

2 **Complete the table with language from the conversations in Exercise 1.**

Saying you like something:	That's a really nice jacket.
Saying something is good for the person who is wearing it:	
Being pleased that someone compliments you:	

3 Choose six words from the list to match the things in the picture.

corduroy	plastic
cotton	polyester
denim	silk
leather	wool
nylon	

a ....
b ....
c ....
d ....
e ....
f ....

4 Complete the conversations with the lines from the box.

- It was a present from my husband.
- It was given to me by my aunt.
- No I don't think so. It's from Korea.
- Oh thanks.
- Oh yes. So it's a Swiss watch then?
- Well it looks good with that suit. What's it made of?
- Where did you get it?

a SUSAN: That's a really nice jacket.
MARY: (1) ....
SUSAN: Not at all! Where did you get it?
MARY: (2) ....
SUSAN: He chose well. It really suits you.

b RACHEL: I like your shirt.
TOM: (1) ....
RACHEL: (2) ....
TOM: I don't know. Cotton, I expect.

c BILL: That's a really nice watch.
GRAHAM: I'm glad you like it.
BILL: (1) ....
GRAHAM: From that shop in Constitution Square, you know, the one opposite the cinema.
BILL: (2) ....
GRAHAM: (3) ....

Pronunciation: showing interest

5 Listen to the man's responses on Track 30. Write a line under the main stress in the following phrases. The first one is done for you.

a That's fantastic.
b How interesting!
c That is interesting.
d Oh, really?
e You're thinking of getting married?
f You live in Birmingham?

6 Say the sentences like the speaker on Track 30.

C Check out

Word list

accuse be born bring up capture conquer corduroy cotton crown defeat denim die disguise divorced educate elect escape execute guilty imprison inherit leather marry nylon pirate plastic poison polyester prison sentence (v) shoot silk soldier stab wool

1 Decide which words in the word list have (a) a positive feeling, (b) a negative feeling, or (c) a neutral feeling, and complete the columns.

a Words with a positive feeling	b Words with a negative feeling	c Words with a neutral feeling
....	....	....
....	....	....
....	....	....

Pronunciation: syllables and stresses

2 a Circle all the words in the word list with two or more syllables. Then underline where the stress falls on each of these words. Which syllable is most often stressed: the first one, the last one, or the one before the last one?

When you have finished, listen to Track 31 and check.

b Complete the chart with words from the word list that include the letter 'o'. How is it pronounced in each case? Which 'o' word in the word list doesn't fit in any of the boxes? Practise saying the words.

/ɔː/ - *worn*	/ɒ/ - *song*	/ɔɪ/ - *boy*	/ə/ - *photograph*	/əʊ/- *Oh!*	/uː/- *pool*

Listen to Track 32 and check.

3 Look at the words in the word list box.

a List the words that can be both nouns and verbs: ....

....

b List the words that can be both nouns and adjectives. What word family do these words belong to?

....

UNIT 7

A Multi-word verbs

1 **Which of the following would you find most difficult to *give up*?**

- chocolate
- coffee
- going to clubs
- listening to music
- shopping
- watching TV
- sugar
- something else: ....

Using a dictionary: phrasal verb types

2 **Look at extracts from the dictionary entries for *give away*, *give back*, *give in to*, *give off*, *give out*.**

give sb/sth **away** *phr v*
1 to give something to someone because you do not want or need it for yourself: *I gave most of my books away when I left college.* | **[+to]** *Give your old clothes away to a thrift shop.*

give sth ⇔ **back** *phr v*
1 to give something to the person it belongs to or the person who gave it to you: *This isn't your money and you must give it back.* | *Of course you can have a look at it, as long as you give it back.* | **give sth back to sb** *I'll give the keys back to you tomorrow morning.* | **give sb sth ⇔ back** *Her ex-husband refused to give her back any of her old photos and letters.*

give off sth *phr v*
to produce a smell, light, heat, a sound etc: *The wood gave off a sweet, perfumed smell as it burned.* | *Try not to breathe in the fumes given off by the paint.*

give out *phr v*
1 give sth ⇔ out to give something to each person in a group; **hand out**: *Can you give the drinks out, please?* | **[+to]** *Students were giving out leaflets to everyone on the street.*

give in to sth *phr v*
to no longer try to stop yourself from doing something you want to do: *Don't give in to the temptation to argue back.* | *If you feel the urge for a cigarette, try not to give in to it.*

Which of them can be split up, with the object sometimes going between the verb (*give*) and the particle (*away*, *back*, *in to* etc.)? Which of them cannot be split up?

a (can be split up:) ....

b (cannot be split up:) ....

3 **Now look at the entry for *cut* in your dictionary, and answer these questions.**

a How many phrasal verbs are made with this verb? ....

....

b Which of them (if any) can have the object between the verb and the particle? ....

....

4 Look at these resolutions that people made last New Year's Eve (December 31st). Replace the phrases in italics with one of the phrasal verbs on the right. The first one is done for you.

break up with	make a go of	take up
cut down on	put in	working out
get round to	see about	
go on	set up	

a 'I'm going to *make* my business *successful*.'

I'm going to make a go of my business.

b 'I'm going to *begin the hobby of* weight training.'

....

c 'We're going to *continue training* at the gym.' (two phrasal verbs)..............................

d 'We're going to *create* a new business.'

....

e 'I'm going to *finally start* building a new kitchen.'

....

f 'I'm going to *finish my relationship with* my girlfriend.'..............................

g 'I'm going to *investigate the possibilities of* finding a job.'

....

h 'We're going to *reduce* the amount of wasted paper in the office.'..............................

i 'I'm going to *spend* more hours at the factory.'

....

5 Read the following description of the four different types of phrasal verb.

DIFFERENT TYPES OF PHRASAL VERBS

Type 1 – The verb takes no *object*:
Flight 301 has already ***taken off****.*

Type 2 – The object can go after the phrasal verb or between the *verb* and the *particle*:
Can you ***pick up*** *Mr Smith? Can you* ***pick*** *Mr Smith* ***up****?*
However, if the object is a *pronoun* (***me, you, him*** etc.) it can only go between the verb and particle:
Can you ***pick*** *him* ***up****?* Not: ~~*Can you pick up him?*~~

Type 3 – The object always comes after the particle:
I'm not very good at ***looking after*** *children.*
Not: ~~*I'm not very good at looking children after*~~.

Type 4 – The phrasal verb has two or more *particles*, and the object always comes after the particles:
Oh no! We've ***run out of*** *petrol.*

Which type are the phrasal verbs from Exercise 4?

a Type 1: ....

b Type 2: ....

c Type 3: ....

d Type 4: ....

6 Choose nine verbs from Exercises 1–4 to complete the following text.

JULIO'S DILEMMA

Six months ago Julio Gonzalez and his sister Marcia both worked for a car company. They were both fed up with their jobs, and then Marcia **(a)** .... her boyfriend of three years – and started to feel very unhappy. She needed something to make her feel better, so one day she said to her brother, 'Look, I can't **(b)** .... working at a boring job, and I don't like feeling unhappy. I want to do something new. Let's start our own business. I'm sure we could **(c)** .... it if we worked hard.'

And so they **(d)** .... a car repair business. At first everything went well. Julio **(e)** .... about 60 hours a week. Occasionally he would **(f)** .... seeing a film with his wife or going out for a drink with his friend Hedley, and that was about all. It was just work, work, work. But then one day, after a conversation with his friend, he **(g)** .... golf – and now he spends more and more time at the golf course.

His sister and wife are both furious. 'With you it's either work or golf! What kind of a life is that?' his wife complained to him last night. 'If you don't **(h)** .... one or the other, I'm going to go on strike, and you can run this house and this family by yourself. See how you like that!'

Marcia's sister is just as dramatic. **(i)** '.......... golf,' she told him yesterday. 'We've got a factory to run!'

So that's Julio's dilemma. Work, golf, his wife and his sister. As he said to his friend Hedley, 'What am I going to do?'

B Making promises

1 Answer the following questions about marriage in your country.

a Where do most people get married? ....

b What happens during the marriage ceremony? ....

....

c What words are used, and what do they mean in English?

....

....

2 Listen to Track 33 and match the extracts (1–4) with the pictures (a–d) below.

a ....

b ....

c ....

d ....

3 Listen to Track 33 again and complete the table with Ben and Mariah's wedding vows.

	a I promise to:	b I agree to:	c I'll:	d I give you my word that:
Ben				
Mariah				

4 **Choose the appropriate ending from the box and write the second part of the following sentences (a–j). The first one is done for you.**

... and obey you forever.

... be there on time – for once!

... but I don't promise to make a particularly good job of it.

... but you have to organise the drinks.

... get to class late again. Honestly.

... if you'll do all the cooking.

... promise not to play such loud music in the evenings.

... rude to all my friends when I invite them round to our flat?

... the bathroom tidy, at least?

... you'll never misbehave in class again?

a Do you promise not to be rude to all my friends when I invite them round to our flat?

b I agree to give you more time to yourself, but you have to ....

c I give you my word that I'll never ....

d I promise that I'll ....

e I promise to love ....

f I'll get some glasses, ...

g Let's make a bargain. I'll do all the washing up ....

h Look, I'll agree to paint the walls in the kitchen ....

i Will you agree to keep ....

j Will you give me your word that ....

Pronunciation: how sounds change in contracted forms

5 **Listen to the following sentences on Track 34. Does the sound of *I* (/aɪ/) change in the examples? Why?**

I will do it tomorrow. / I'll do it tomorrow.
I will have that coffee now, please. / I'll have that coffee now, please.
I will answer the telephone. / I'll answer the telephone.
I will talk to you later. / I'll talk to you later.
I will be home at nine. / I'll be home at nine.
I will never forget this. / I'll never forget this.

....

6 **Say the contracted sentences in the same way as the speakers on Track 34.**

C Check out

Word list

agree to break up with
cut down on get round to
give (somebody) my word
give away give in to
give off give out
give up go on look after
make a go of pick up
promise to put in
resolution see about
set up take off take up
work out

1 Choose one word or one phrase from the word list that is important to you and think why you have chosen it. Here is an example:

'look after', because I like looking after animals

Pronunciation

2 Complete the table with words from the word list that have the following sounds.

a day /eɪ/	b cow /aʊ/	c so /əʊ/

Listen to Track 35 and check.

Can you think of any other words to add to the table? Write them in the correct column.

3 Listen to this sentence said in different ways on Track 36. Underline the word that is stressed most strongly in each case.

a I promise I'll be at your house by four o'clock.
b I promise I'll be at your house by four o'clock.
c I promise I'll be at your house by four o'clock.
d I promise I'll be at your house by four o'clock.
e I promise I'll be at your house by four o'clock.

4 Listen to Track 36 again and match these meanings with the sentences in Exercise 3. The first one is done for you.

1 I don't know about anyone else. [d]
2 I really, really do promise. [ ]
3 I'm not going to anyone else's house. [ ]
4 Not at any other time – not later anyway. [ ]
5 Not at your office. [ ]

5 Listen Track 36 and repeat the sentences in the same way.

UNIT 8

A Anti-social activities

1 **Complete the following opinions with an appropriate verb from the box.**

drive	light	put up
drop	listen to	ride
have	make	smoke
let	paint	use

a .... litter.

b spray-.............................. the walls.

c .... posters everywhere.

d .... their dogs foul the footpath.

e .... a lot of noise in a quiet area late at night.

f .... a walkman near other people.

g .... bicycles on the pavement.

h .... an over-sensitive car alarm.

i .... a smoky bonfire in the middle of the day.

j .... too fast in built-up areas.

k .... mobile phones on the train.

l .... in public places.

Using a dictionary: transitive and intransitive verbs

2 **Look at the dictionary entries for *light*, *paint* and *shout*. Do these verbs always take an object? How do you know?**

light[3] /laɪt/ (past tense and past participle **lit** /lɪt/) verb ★★★
1 [T] to make something start to burn: *Amy lit a cigarette.* —picture → BURN **1a.** [I] to start to burn: *The fire won't light if the wood is wet.*
2 light or **light up** [T often passive] to make a place brighter by giving it light: **+by** *The room was lit by candlelight.* ♦ **dimly/badly/brightly lit** *The room was dimly lit.*
3 [T] if you light someone's way, you use a light to lead them through a dark place
light a fire under sb *mainly AmE informal* to make someone work harder

paint[1] /peɪnt/ verb ★★★
1 [I/T] to put paint onto something to change its colour: *She was painting her nails.* ♦ *They followed the white arrows painted on the road.* ♦ *Wash the walls before you start to paint.*
2 [I/T] to create a picture of something using paints: *I* [illegible]

shout[1] S2 W2 /ʃaʊt/ v
1 [I,T] to say something very loudly; → **scream, yell**: *There's no need to shout! I can hear you!* | **[+at]** *I wish you'd stop shouting at the children.* | **[+for]** *We could hear them **shouting for help**.* | *'Watch out!' she shouted, as the car started to move.* | **shout sth at sb** *He was shouting insults at the lorry driver.* | **shout sth to sb** *'He's down here!' she shouted to Alison.*
2 shout in pain/anger/frustration etc *BrE* to call out loudly; **scream** *AmE*: *My brother shouted in pain as the ball hit him.*
3 shout sth from the rooftops to tell everyone about something because you want everyone to know about it

3 Decide whether the following verbs *Always* (A), *Never* (N) or *Sometimes* (S) take an object. Check in a dictionary to see if you were right.

bring [ ]
come [ ]
colour [ ]
drive [ ]
drop [ ]
enjoy [ ]
fall [ ]
open [ ]

4 Using words from Exercises 1 and 3, write instructions for the following signs. The first one has been done for you.

a Don't bring food into the library.

b ....

c ....

d ....

e ....

f ....

g ....

h ....

Pronunciation: different accents

5 Look at the following words. What do they mean? Now listen to the words said first by an American and then by a British speaker on Track 37. Is the pronunciation the *Same* (S) or *Different* (D)?

a advertisement [ ]
b brochure [ ]
c cinema [ ]
d controversy [ ]
e entertainer [ ]
f interesting [ ]
g lieutenant [ ]
h officer [ ]
i opinion [ ]
j simultaneous [ ]

6 When the pronunciation is different, what is the main difference in each case? Say the words using either American or British pronunciation.

B Permission

1 Before you listen to Track 38, look at the pictures and complete the conversations with one of the lines in the box.

I'd rather you didn't.
No, sorry. We operate a 'no dogs' policy.
No, sir. I'm afraid taking photographs is strictly forbidden.
Not at all. We'd love to meet her.
Sure. Help yourself.
Yes, certainly.

a 'Can I sit here, please?'

'...'

b 'Can I use my camera in here?'

'...'

c 'Are dogs allowed in here?'

'...'

d 'Is it OK if I use my mobile phone in here?'

'...'

e 'Is it all right if I take one of these?'

'...'

f 'Do you mind if I bring my sister to the party?'

'...'

Listen to Track 38. Were you correct?

2 Complete the boxes with phrases from the conversations in Exercise 1.

a Asking for permission	b Saying 'yes':	c Saying 'no':
Do you mind if I ...?		

3 Complete the following dialogues using the expressions above. Write one word in each gap.

a '.................. .... mind if I arrive late?'
'I'd rather ....'

b '.................. .... right if I sit here?'
'I'm sorry sir, but sitting on the exhibits is strictly ....'

c ' .... I have a serviette?'
'Sure. .... yourself. '

d 'Do .... if I take your picture?'
'No, not .... Go ahead.'

4 Put the words of these conversation lines in order. Pay attention to the punctuation and add capital letters where necessary. The first one is done for you.

a A: ? /allowed / are / children / here / in
Are children allowed in here?
B: course / of / , / . / sure
Sure, of course.

b A: take / here / I / if / is / ? / it / photograph/ a / OK
....
B: didn't / I'd / . / rather / you
....

c A: all / bring / dog / here / ? / I / if / in / is / it / my / right
....
B: but / , / keep / . / it / it's / quiet / yes / okay
....

d A: do / I / if / mind / ? / photographs / some / take / you
....
B: afraid / I'm / not / . / possible / that's
....

e A: bring / can / the / ? / friend / I / my / to / party /
....
B: come / she's / sure / . / . / . / to / welcome
....

f A: can / ? / I / of / one / programmes / take / these
....
B: help / . / . / sure / yourself
....

C Check out

Word list

alarm   anti-social   barbecue   bonfire   built-up area
graffiti   here   library   over-sensitive   pavement   smoky
spray-paint (v)   to drop litter   to let your dog foul the footpath
to make a lot of noise   to put up posters   walkman

1 Imagine that you live in an English-speaking country. Which five words or phrases from the word list would you use most?

....

....

Pronunciation

2 Find a word in the word list with the same sounds as each of the following words, and write them in the correct column.

/aɪ/ – fine	/aɪə/ – liar	/ɪə/- fear

Listen to Track 39 and check.

Try to add more words of your own in each column in the table.

3 Write sentences that accuse people of performing anti-social acts. Use the words from the word list, like this example:

You dropped litter on the pavement.

Mark where you would put the stresses in the sentences, like this:

You dropped litter on the pavement.

....

....

....

....

....

Now read them out as accusations.

4 Listen to Track 40 and then divide the words on the left into two lists. The first one is done for you.

- amazing
- certainly
- exactly
- forbidden
- graffiti
- occasion
- opinion
- permission
- sensitive
- signature

List 1 (stress on the second syllable):
amazing
List 2 (stress on the first syllable):

Listen to Track 40 again and say the words.

UNIT 9

A Body language

Using a dictionary: verb collocation

1 Look at this dictionary entry for *clench*.

> **clench** /klentʃ/ *v* [T] **1 clench your fists/teeth/jaw etc** to hold your hands, teeth etc together tightly, usually because you feel angry or determined: *Jody was pacing the sidelines, her fists clenched.* **2** to hold something tightly in your hand or between your teeth: *a cigar clenched between his teeth*

a Does the verb always take an object? How do you know?

....

....

b What nouns is it used with most often?

....

....

2 Using a dictionary, write a noun from the second list that is often used with these verbs. Sometimes there is more than one answer.

Verbs	Nouns
a clench + ...	arms
b cross + ...	ear
c fold + ...	eyebrows
d nod + ...	finger(s)
e point + ...	fist
f raise + ...	hand(s)
g scratch + ...	head
h shake + ...	legs
i shrug + ...	neck
j wag + ...	shoulders
k wave + ...	teeth

3 Look at the picture and write the correct names in the gaps.

a ...John... has folded his arms.
b .... is clenching his fist.
c .... is wagging its tail.
d .... has crossed his legs.
e .... is raising her eyebrows.
f .... is pointing at someone.
g .... is waving her arm.
h .... is nodding his head.
i .... is scratching his head.
j .... is shrugging her shoulders.

4 Complete the sentences using a verb and noun pair from Exercise 2. Change the verb to the *-ing form* and add a possessive adjective (e.g. *his*, *her*). The first one is done for you.

a 'Get your dog out of my garden!,' Mr King shouted, ...shaking his fist.......... .
b 'Yes, you're right,' Louise agreed, ...
c 'Look, it's over there,' Juan said, ...
d 'I don't really care,' Carla said, ...
e 'This is a really comfortable chair!' the customer said, ...
f 'Goodbye,' Frank said, ...
g 'You are a very naughty girl!' the teacher said, ...
h 'Oh dear. I just don't understand how it works,' the technician said, ...
i 'Ooh! That's a surprise,' Barbara said, ...
j 'I must try to be patient,' Janine thought, ...

Pronunciation: how many syllables?

5 Listen to Track 41 and write down how many syllables you hear for each word.

a different ....
b interest ....
c usually ....
d consciously ....
e general ....
f intimacy ....
g subconsciously ....
h relaxation ....

6 Write down three three-syllable words and three four-syllable words from this unit.

a (three-syllable words:) ....
b (four-syllable words:) ....

B Directing people's actions

1 Look at the pictures and read the conversations. Put the expressions from the box into the correct gaps in the two conversations.

Anything else	shake your fist
It's difficult to say	shrug your shoulders
easy to say	do this scene
fold your arms	what do I do
folding your arms	

a

STEVE (THE ACTOR): How do I play this scene?

MR GOLDSTEIN (THE DIRECTOR): (1) .... I think you're probably quite angry in this bit.

STEVE: OK. So what do you recommend?

MR GOLDSTEIN: I think you can come in and (2) .... at Caspar as you start talking.

STEVE: (3) .... ?

MR GOLDSTEIN: Well you could (4) .... then, so that you go on looking angry.

STEVE: Is this what you had in mind?

MR GOLDSTEIN: Yes, that's the type of thing.

b

MARK (THE ACTOR): How do you want me to (1) .... ?

MS HOWARD (THE DIRECTOR): That's not (2) .... I think you're probably a bit bored in this scene.

STEVE: OK. So (3) .... ?

MS HOWARD: Well I think you can show boredom by (4) .... , or crossing your legs when you sit down.

STEVE: Is that all?

MS HOWARD: Well, you could (5) .... when she talks to you.

STEVE: Like this?

MS HOWARD: Yes, that's the kind of thing.

Listen to Track 42 and check your answers.

2 Write phrases from Exercise 1 in the appropriate box. The first one is done for you.

Asking for advice:	How do you want me to ...
Expressing doubt:	
Giving advice:	
Checking you have understood correctly:	
Agreeing with an action:	

3 What words can go in the gaps?

a How do you .... me to do this?

b I .... you should wave your arm.

c Is this what you had in .... ?

d I .... you can play this scene quietly.

e .... else?

f That's not .... to say.

g Yes, that's the .... of thing that you should do.

h Well, you .... fold your arms.

i You .... raise your eyebrow when the camera looks at you.

4 Choose a phrase or word from the box to complete these phrases.

and cross your legs.
else?
me to play this scene?
would show you are relaxed.
the kind of thing.
this?
to say.
scratch your ear or something.

a Anything ....

b It's difficult ....

c How do you want ....

d I reckon you could ....

e Like ....

f Well yes. You could sit down ....

g Yes, that's ....

h That ....

5 Now use the sentences in Exercise 4 and write them as a conversation.

ACTOR: ....

DIRECTOR: ....

ACTOR: ....

DIRECTOR: ....

ACTOR: ....

DIRECTOR: ....

C Check out

1 Find at least three words from the word list that have more than one meaning.

....

....

Word list

arm body language clench consciously cross (v) ear eyebrows finger fist fold gesture head intimacy leg neck nod point protect puzzled raise relaxation scratch shake shoulders shrug subconsciously teeth to tell the truth wag wave

Pronunciation

2 a How many different sounds do each of the following words have? Which is the easiest/most difficult word to pronounce?

1 cross .....4.....
2 finger ....
3 indifference ....
4 puzzled ....
5 strangers ....
6 truth ....

Listen to Track 43 and check.

b Find words in the word list with four syllables. Where is the main stress?

....

....

....

....

Listen to Track 44 and check.

What other words can you think of with the same stress patterns?

....

....

....

....

....

....

....

3 **Read the following phrases, sentences and questions and say them to yourself. Think carefully where the stress goes.**

a	Are you waving at me?	
b	Don't raise your eyebrows at me!	
c	Don't shake your fist at me!	
d	I am telling the truth.	
e	I can't be absolutely sure.	
f	I quite agree with you.	
g	I'm pleased to see you.	
h	It's so nice to see you.	
i	Stop biting your nails!	1

Now listen to Track 45. Number the phrases, sentences and questions in the order of the stress and intonation patterns you hear. The first one is done for you.

UNIT 10

A Technology and computers

1 Write the letter of the correct item next to the words. The first one is done for you.

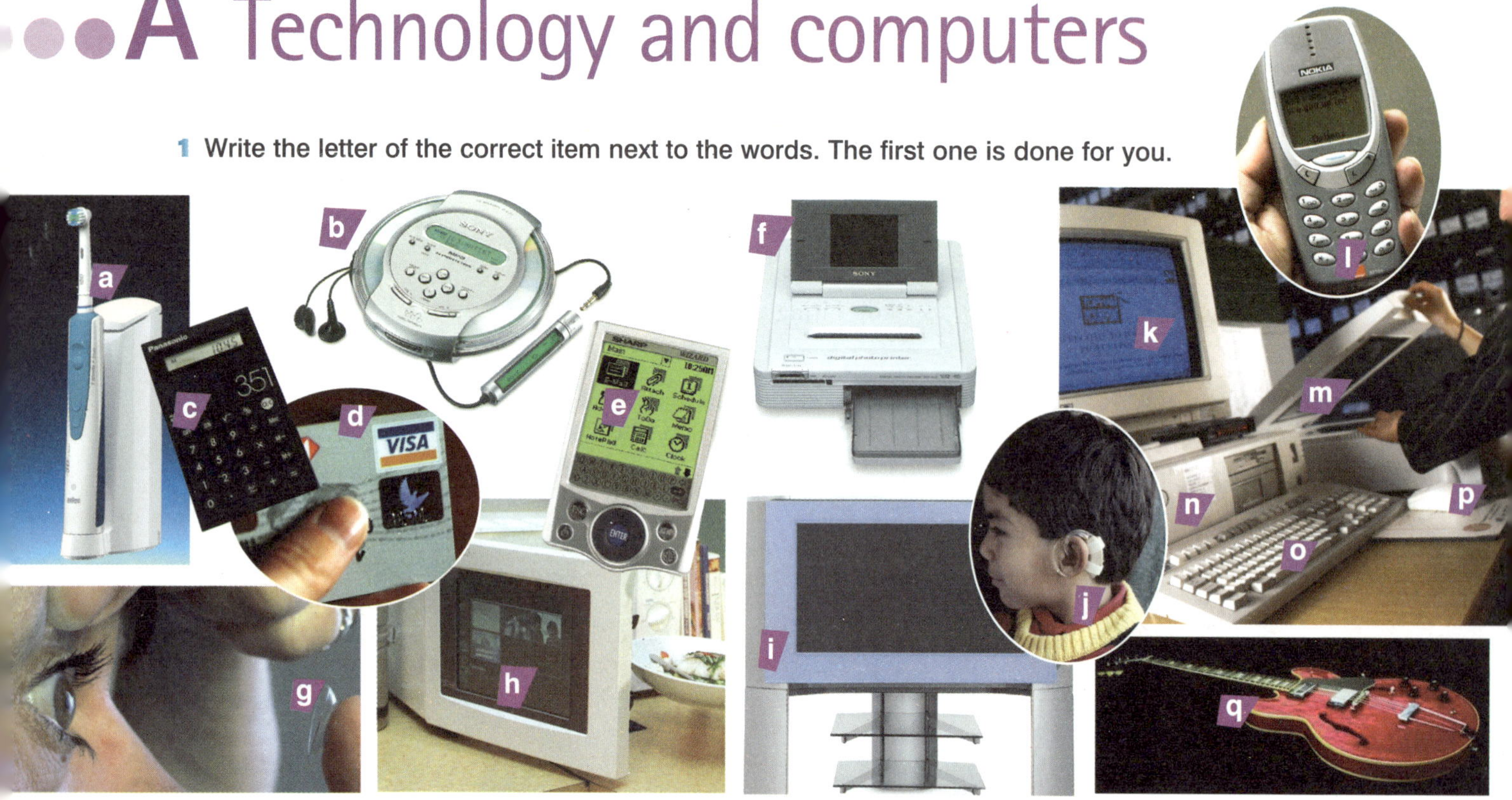

calculator	[...c...]	electric toothbrush	[........]	monitor	[........]
computer	[........]	electronic personal organiser	[........]	mouse	[........]
contact lenses	[........]	keyboard	[........]	personal stereo	[........]
credit card	[........]	microwave oven	[........]	printer	[........]
hearing aid	[........]	mobile phone	[........]	scanner	[........]
electric guitar	[........]			television	[........]

2 Using a dictionary if you need to, complete the sentences with words or phrases from the box.

computer viruses
crashes
emails
bug
go online
website

a You can't .... if your brother is using the telephone line to talk to his friends.

b Many people send and receive .... rather than telephoning or using 'snail mail' (letter post).

c These days you can buy things on the Internet by going to a company's ....

d Sometimes the computer ...., and then it's impossible to use it. You usually have to switch it off and start again.

e Some people create ...., which infect any computer they arrive at. They are very dangerous and can destroy everything on the hard disk.

f If a computer programme has a ...., it won't work properly.

Using a dictionary: different meanings, different grammar

3 Look at the dictionary entry for *application*.

a How many different meanings are given?

....

b Is the noun countable (like *table* – we can say *a table*, *two tables* etc.) or uncountable (like *furniture* – we can't say ~~*two furnitures*~~)? How do you know?

....

....

c What words follow *application* in meaning 1?

....

d What do you know about meanings 3 and 4? When is *application* used for these meanings?

....

....

application /ˌæplɪˈkeɪʃn/ noun ★★★

1 request for sth
2 particular use sth has
3 computer software
4 effort/determination
5 putting sth onto surface

1 [C/U] a formal request for permission to do or have something: **+for** *His application for membership of the club was rejected.* ♦ **application to do sth** *The hospital submitted a planning application to build four new wards.* ♦ **make / submit / put in an application** *I'm supposed to submit my application before the end of the week.* ♦ **grant / approve an application** *The building society has approved their mortgage application.* **1a.** a written request for a job or a place at a college, university etc: *The university welcomes applications from mature students.* ♦ *a letter of application*
2 [C] a particular use that something has: *the practical applications of this technology* **2a.** [U] the use of a particular method, process, law etc: *He pioneered the application of scientific techniques to police work.*
3 [C] *computing* a piece of computer software that is designed to do a particular job
4 [U] *formal* hard work and determination that you put into something for a long period: *With the right degree of application and dedication the team should win a medal.*
5 [C/U] the process of putting a substance such as paint or glue onto a surface

4 Put the following computer operations in the correct place in the flow chart. The first one is done for you.

- Close the application.
- Open the application you want.
- Print your work.
- Save your work on to the hard disk.
- Switch off the computer, the monitor and the printer.
- Switch on the computer, the monitor and the printer.
- Work.

a Switch on the computer, the monitor and the printer.
↓
b
↓
c
↓
d
↓
e
↓
f
↓
g

B Asking for technical help

1 Read all the conversations and then decide where these questions and replies should go in the conversations. The first one has been done for you.

do you know how to connect up to the Internet? ......b1......
Have you checked the connection ....
How may I help you? ....
No. Do you think that will help? ....
OK. I'll give it a try. ....
Really? ....
Thanks. That's great! ....
Well, I can't get my personal organiser to work with my computer. ....

a

RON: Computer Helpline, Ron speaking.
KARL: Oh, hello. Can you help me?
RON: What's the problem?
KARL: (1) ....
RON: OK. Have you checked the batteries in your organiser?
KARL: Yes, of course.
RON: (2) .... at the back of your computer?
KARL: (3) ....
RON: Do I think it will help? Well why don't you try and see?

b

RACHEL: Hello. Computer Helpline. Rachel speaking. What seems to be the problem?
JIM: Umm, well I know this is silly, but (1) .... ?
RACHEL: What system are you using?
JIM: It's an Apple Mac.
RACHEL: OK. Do you have an Internet icon on your screen? Like a globe?
JIM: Yes. Yes, I do.
RACHEL: Well then just click on the icon and you're away.
JIM: OK, ... oh yes. (2) ....
RACHEL: You're welcome.

c

MIKE: Hi, Computer Helpline. My name's Mike. (1) .... ?
MILLIE: This thing is driving me crazy!
MIKE: Hold on! What's the problem?
MILLIE: Well, my computer seems to have crashed.
MIKE: How exactly?
MILLIE: Well, I can't move anything. Even the cursor just sticks in the same place.
MIKE: OK, well the best thing to do is to switch off and start again.
MILLIE: (2) ....
MIKE: Yes, really. That's what I would do.
MILLIE: (3) .... Thanks.
MIKE: No problem.

Now listen to Track 46. Were you correct?

2 **Put the following lines from the conversations in the right columns. The first one has been done for you.**

Do you think that will help?
Can you help me?
Do you know how to connect up to the Internet?
Have you checked the batteries?
Just click on the icon.
OK. I'll give it a try.
Really?
Thanks.
That's great.
That's what I would do.
The best thing to do is to switch off and start again.
This thing is driving me crazy.
Why don't you try and see?
What seems to be the problem?

a Asking for help/stating a problem:	b Giving help/advice:	c Responding to help/advice:
		Do you think that will help?

Pronunciation: fluent speech

3 **Listen to the two speakers on Track 47. Which one do you think speaks more fluently, the man or the woman?** ....

4 **When the more fluent speaker is talking on Track 47, which words run into each other and change their sounds? When words run into each other use a curved line (‿). When sounds change, use a straight line (—).**

a Can you help me?
b What seems to be the problem?
c Have you checked the batteries?
d Do you know how to use this answerphone?
e What is the problem?
f What do I do now?

5 **Say the questions like the woman on Track 47.**

6 Write the replies (in the box) that match with the sentences. Use each reply once only.

Is it plugged in?
You're welcome.
Sure. Just press the red button and record your message.
The best thing to do would be to call the garage.
Well, that's what I would do.
Why? What seems to be the problem?

a 'Do you know how to use this answerphone?'
'..'

b 'Do you think it will work?'
'..'

c 'My car won't start.' '..'

d 'My iron doesn't work. It's not even hot.'
'..'

e 'Thanks very much for your help.'
'..'

f 'This photocopier is driving me crazy.'
'..'

7 Complete the conversation below, putting one word in each gap.

LAUREN: Software solutions. Lauren speaking. (**a**) .... I help you?

CALLER: Yes please. Well, I hope you can.

LAUREN: What seems to be the (**b**) ....?

CALLER: I don't seem to be able to print out the document I'm working on.

LAUREN: Your printer won't work?

CALLER: No.

LAUREN: Are you (**c**) .... you've switched it on?

CALLER: Of course I'm sure.

LAUREN: I'm sorry, but you (**d**) .... what people are like. Sometimes some people think they've switched it on but they haven't.

CALLER: OK. OK.

LAUREN: So when you (**e**) .... on the printer icon, what (**f**) ....?

CALLER: Well, nothing happens.

LAUREN: Nothing at all?

CALLER: Well, it just says 'printer can not be found' all the time, but that's ridiculous.

LAUREN: OK, have you looked (**g**) .... the printer folder?

CALLER: Yes, and it says 'preparing to print' and then I (**h**) .... that 'printer can not be found' message again.

LAUREN: I see.

CALLER: It's driving me (**i**) .... I've got to finish printing off an essay – or my tutor will kill me.

LAUREN: What about going to the control panel and checking you've selected the right printer. (**j**) .... you done that?

CALLER: Yes, yes of course.

LAUREN: Well then, I can't tell (**k**) ....the problem is from here, really.

CALLER: Please (**l**) .... go away. You can't just leave me alone. You've got to help me.

LAUREN: All right. I tell you what. The best (**m**) .... to do is to switch off everything and (**n**) .... all over again.

CALLER: OK, but will you stay on the line while I do that?

LAUREN: All right, if you hurry.

CALLER: Right, I've (**o**) .... off the computer, and now I'm going to switch off the printer, and … umm … oh … umm … oh dear. The printer … you see it wasn't … oh dear, I think I've been a bit stupid.

LAUREN: Sorry?

CALLER: Listen, you've (**p**) .... very helpful. Honestly. Thanks and everything. Goodbye.

LAUREN: No problem. Goodbye. What was all that about?

C Check out

1 Look at the words in the word list. Underline the words that are connected with computers.

Which of them are like words in your language? Which are completely different?

....

....

....

....

....

Word list

calculator computer computer bug computer virus contact lenses crash (of a computer) credit card disk electric guitar electric toothbrush electronic personal organiser emails go online hard disk keyboard microwave oven mobile phone modem monitor personal stereo printer scanner television the computer's crashed website

Pronunciation

2 a Complete the table with words from the word list that match the stress pattern. The circles represent the syllables. The large circle represents the stressed syllable.

1 oOo	2 Ooo	3 ooOo	4 Oooo
electric		television	

Listen to Track 48 and check.

b Find examples of words from the word list with the following consonant clusters.

1 /kr/ cricket	2 /sk/ school	3 /tr/ travel

Listen to Track 49 and check.

Say the words. Are any of the clusters hard to pronounce?

3 Listen to Track 50 and underline the stressed syllable(s).

a Thank you.
b Thank you.
c Thanks a lot.
d Thank you very much.
e Thank you very much for your help.
f No problem.
g Don't mention it.
h Glad I could help.

Listen to Track 50 again, and repeat the phrases and sentences.

UNIT 11

A The arts

1 Match the pictures with the paragraphs. Put the number of the matching picture in the brackets.

1

2

3

4

a It is a film based on a play called *The Taming of the Shrew* by William Shakespeare. The film is set in an American high school. [ ]

b It is a sculpture by Anthony Gormley. It stands by a motorway in the north of England. There was some controversy about it at first but now it is one of the most popular public works of art in Britain. [ ]

c It is a novel by Stephen King that tells the story of a writer. He has an accident and is then kidnapped by a crazy woman who admires his work. She keeps him prisoner and nearly kills him. [ ]

d It is a play by Ray Lawler about migrant workers in Australia. Many people see it as the first great work of Australian theatre. It has been performed all over the world since its premiere in 1957. [ ]

2 Complete the gaps in the table with the words or phrases in blue from Exercise 1.

It is a painting / (a) .... by (name of artist/sculptor).

It is (b) .... novel / story written by (name of writer).

It is (c) .... Italy. / New York. / the twentieth century.

It is (d) .... migrant workers.

It tells (e) .... of two people who are in love but don't know it.

3 **Write the number of the questions about plays and films in the appropriate columns in the table below.**

1 What are the best bits in the film?
2 What kind of play is it?
3 Who wrote it?
4 What part does X play in the film?
5 What's the story of the film?
6 Who directed the film/play?
7 Who are the main characters in the film?
8 Who's in it?

a Plot:	b Type of play or film:	c Actors:	d Characters:	e Memorable scenes:	f Writer or director:

g Which of the questions (1 – 8) can you also ask about books if you use 'book' instead of 'play' or 'film'? ....

4 **Complete the sentences with the words in the box.**

action
animated
autobiography
biography
comedy
comic
detective
historical
horror
musical
opera
romance
romantic comedies
science
thrillers
tragedy
war
westerns

a A .... novel makes you laugh. So does a .... in the theatre.

b A book about love and relationships is called a .... Funny films where boy and girl fall in love in the end are called ....

c A play which ends in sadness and disaster is a ....

d A play with singing and music is a ....

e A show with classical music, an orchestra and singers who do not use microphones is a called an ....

f A story, in which a clever person discovers who the murderer is, is a .... story.

g Books that are exciting because there is a lot of action in them are called ....

h Fiction about the future is called .... fiction.

i Films about cowboys and Native Americans are called ....

j Films about war are called .... films.

k Films that frighten people are called .... films.

l Films with a lot of action (fights etc.) are called .... films.

m If someone writes a book about their own life, we call it an .... If they write about someone else's life we call it a ....

n Stories about the past are called .... novels.

o When people draw pictures for a film we call it an .... film.

Now copy and complete the table in Exercise 3 with information about your favourite book or play or film.

Using a dictionary: pronunciation, collocation and grammar

5 Look at the dictionary entry for *sculpture* and answer the questions that follow.

sculp·ture /ˈskʌlptʃə $ -ər/ *n* **1** [C,U] an object made out of stone, wood, clay etc by an artist: **[+of]** *a sculpture of an elephant* | *an exhibition of sculpture* **2** [U] the art of making objects out of stone, wood, clay etc

a What is the difference between the pronunciation of *sculpture* in British and American English?

....

b What word often follows *sculpture*? ....

c In the sentence *I prefer painting to sculpture*, is *sculpture* a countable or an uncountable noun?

....

6 Write in questions from Exercise 3 to match the answers. The first one is done for you.

a '*What's your favourite Bond film?*'

'It's Die Another Day.'

b '..'

'For me it was the car chase on the ice and when Bond first sees Jinx. Fantastic!'

c '..'

'Pierce Brosnan and Halle Berry.'

d '..'

'She (Halle Berry) is the character called Jinx.'

e '..'

'It's a Bond film of course – action, adventure, all that kind of thing.'

f '..'

'The two main characters in the film are, well, James Bond, of course, and then a character called Jinx. She's different from a lot of other Bond girls. She's quite a strong person herself.'

g '..'

'There's no real story. It's about someone who wants to take over the world. They always are.'

B Reacting to what people say

1 Listen to Track 51 and fill in the missing parts of the conversation.

NANCY: How was the film?

JIM: It was a disaster. Halfway through they stopped it and told us we had to leave.

NANCY: (a) ....

JIM: Well, yes. We all had to go out into the street, even though it was raining.

NANCY: (b) ....

JIM: No, it certainly wasn't. I got soaked. But then, when we were allowed back, they started the film again and offered all of us free tickets to any film for the next month.

NANCY: (c) ....

JIM: I certainly was. Would you like to come to the next film with me?

2 Complete the following replies with words and phrases from the box. The first one is done for you.

been easy	much fun
exhausted	wonderful
hurt yourself	

a You were so lucky! That must have been ...wonderful... .

b After all that effort, you must have been ....

c That can't have .... I don't think I could have done it.

d That was a really crazy thing to do. You might have ....

e That couldn't have been ....

3 Respond to the following stories with replies like those in Exercise 2. The first one has been done for you.

a 'And then I saw it. The summit of Mount Everest.' '...That must have been fantastic!...'

b 'And then suddenly he turned white and fell off his chair – right in front of me!'
'..................'

c 'When the car ran out of petrol I had to walk for three miles to the nearest garage.'
'..................'

d 'We had to get the old piano up the stairs.'
'..................'

e 'When I woke up the house was on fire.'
'..................'

f 'I met my favourite actor in the street yesterday.' '..................'

g 'Last year I won a ticket for the World Cup final in a raffle.'
'..................'

h 'When we got home we discovered that someone had stolen our television.'
'..................'

4 **Write the number of the appropriate reply (on the right) beside the statements on the left.**

a I fell off my bicycle in the middle of the street yesterday, but luckily not in front of a car! [ ]
b Yesterday I had to tell my music teacher that I wasn't going to attend her classes anymore. [ ]
c I left my handbag on the train, but luckily someone gave it to a railway official. [ ]
d I saw a ghost last night! [ ]
e I stayed up all night to finish my homework. [ ]
f I went to a fantastic concert last night. [ ]
g I won a prize for my latest book last week. [ ]
h Our cat died last week. We'd had him for 13 years. [ ]
i Someone took me to see a play in a foreign language that I don't speak. [ ]
j We went walking in the mountains, but nobody had brought a compass and we got completely lost. Luckily a man in a light aeroplane spotted us. [ ]

1 How incredible to get it back. I mean, someone might have stolen it.
2 That can't have been easy. What did she say?
3 That can't have been very interesting.
4 That must have been absolutely wonderful.
5 That must have been frightening.
6 Yes, that was lucky. You might have been killed!
7 Yes, that was lucky. You might have been lost forever.
8 You must have been absolutely devastated. You probably still are.
9 You must be absolutely worn out.
10 You must be really proud of yourself.

Pronunciation: intonation and punctuation

5 **Listen to Track 52 and punctuate the lines in the following conversations. You can use full stops, question marks and exclamation marks.**

a
A: How was the film
B: Fantastic
A: Fantastic
B: Fantastic

b
A: How long do you think the film was?
B: An hour and a half
A: Ha
B: Two hours
A: Ha
B: Two and a half hours
A: Keep going
B: Three hours
A: Three and a half hours
B: Three and a half hours
A: Yes
B: No
A: Yes Three and a half hours
B: Three and a half hours

6 **What helped you to complete Exercise 5? Was it the pronunciation of different words or the intonation (the 'music') the speakers used?**

....

....

Now say the lines in exactly the same way as the speakers on the tape.

C Check out

1 Which words and phrases in the word list did you know when you started the unit? Tick the words that you knew and draw a circle around the words that were new for you. Choose five of the new words and use them in sentences.

....

....

....

....

....

Word list

- action film
- animated film
- autobiography
- biography
- comedy
- detective story
- horror film
- it's a book/film/play about ...
- it's based on
- it's set in
- logical
- musical
- novel
- opera
- painting
- play (n)
- romantic comedy
- science fiction
- sculpture
- story
- thriller
- tragedy
- war film
- western

Pronunciation

2 **a** The letter 'g' can be pronounced in two ways. Find an example of each in the word list.

....

....

Listen to Track 53 and check.

List three other words with each type of 'g' sound.

....

....

b Look at the word list.

1 Write the word with the most syllables and underline the stressed syllable. ....

2 Write the words with four syllables and underline the stressed syllable for each word. ....

Listen to Track 54 and check.

3 Where is the main stress in each of the following comments? Listen to Track 55 and underline the syllable with the main stress in each sentence.

Listen to Track 55 again and repeat the comments.

a You might have hurt yourself.

b You can't have been very pleased.

c That must have been terrifying.

d You could have been in real danger.

e That couldn't have been pleasant.

UNIT 12

A Injuries

1 Look at the picture. Put the words below in the right boxes.

ankle	stomach
collar bone	throat
ear	thumb
elbow	toes
eye	tooth
index finger	waist
little finger	wrist
heel	big toe
knee	thigh
nose	

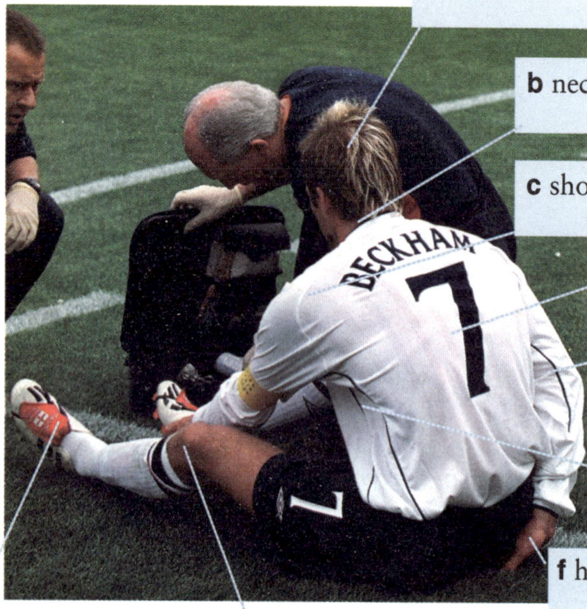

i What is the footballer's problem, do you think? ....

....

Using a dictionary: how a word is used

2 Look at the dictionary entry for *swollen*.

> **swollen**[1] /ˈswəʊlən/ adj ★
> **1** an area of your body that is swollen has increased in size as a result of an injury or illness: *a swollen hand/knee/foot*
> **2** a swollen river or stream contains more water than normal as a result of heavy rain or snow that has MELTED
> **have a swollen head** to think that you are more clever, important etc than you really are because you have been successful at something
> **sw...llen**[2] the past participle of swell

a What part of speech is it?

....

b What can it be used to describe, apart from parts of the body? ....

....

c What is special about someone with a *swollen head*? ....

....

3 Complete the tables using the words from Exercise 1. Two are done for you.

a

earache,	+ ache

Note: with *stomach* and *tummy* (= an informal word for *stomach*) we make two words (*stomach ache*, *tummy ache*). With other words we make one word (e.g. *earache*).

b

1 broken	broken ankle,
2 fractured	
3 sprained	
4 swollen	
5 sore	
6 a pain in the …	

4 Look at the pictures. What's the person's problem? The first one is done for you.

a She's got a stomach ache. ....

d ....

b ....

e ....

c ....

f ....

g ....

....

....

h ....

....

....

i ....

....

....

j ....

....

....

k ....

....

....

Pronunciation: intonation clues

5 a Listen to Track 56. Can you guess the complete football scores? Who won each time?

a Everton 0, Sunderland …
b Aston Villa 2, Sheffield United …
c Liverpool 1, Burnley …
d Newcastle United 2, Manchester United …
e Blackburn Rovers 0, Sheffield Wednesday …
f Arsenal 2, Manchester City …
g Tottenham Hotspur 3, Leeds United …

b Now listen to Track 57 to hear the complete football scores. Were you correct? What helped you decide?

B Asking how someone is

1 **Before you listen to Track 58, put Jane's questions and answers in the right gaps.**

VICKY: Hi Jane, how are you?

JANE: (a) ....

VICKY: Oh, fine, I suppose. You're looking well, by the way.

JANE: (b) ....

VICKY: Good.

JANE: (c) ....

VICKY: Thanks!

JANE: (d) ....

VICKY: It's all right. It's true; I have been a bit under the weather recently. Work, that kind of thing.

JANE: (e) ....

VICKY: Oh, I don't really think I'm up to it. Do you mind?

JANE: (f) ....

1 But what about you? You look terrible.
2 I'm fine. How about you?
3 No sorry, I mean …
4 Oh, poor you. Listen, why not come round after the practice and I'll try and cheer you up.
5 No, not at all. Get well soon.
6 Thanks. I had an infection. I was off work, but I'm better now.

Now listen to Track 58. Were you correct?

2 **Complete the table with language from the conversation in Exercise 1.**

a Asking how someone is or commenting on how they look:	
b Saying how you are or how you have been:	
c Reacting to how someone is:	

Where would you put the following in the table above?

1 I'm fine (now).
2 How awful.
3 I've broken my leg.
4 I heard you'd been ill/in an accident.
5 I've sprained my ankle.
6 I was in an accident.
7 I'm not very well, actually.
8 I've been ill.
9 I've got …
10 Oh, I'm pleased to hear that.
11 That's great.
12 What happened to you?
13 Oh, I'm sorry to hear that.

3 **Which of the following describe a specific illness or problem? Which describe the way you feel? Put the following words and phrases into the correct column (a or b) below.**

a bad back   ill   flu   a migraine   sick
a stomach ache   food poisoning   terrible   a cold
not very well   off-colour

a *to have* (a specific illness/problem):	**b** *to feel:*

4 **Write one word in each gap. The first one is done for you.**

TRACEY: Hi Marlene (a) ....how.... are you?

MARLENE: Oh fine. Well I am now. It's (b) .... to be back.

TRACEY: Yes, I agree. Holidays back at home with your family are pretty stressful.

MARLENE: It's not so much that. I mean my family are pretty wild, it's true, but this time it (c) .... really their fault.

TRACEY: Why? What was the (d) .... ?

MARLENE: I got ill. Caught flu or something, so I was in (e) .... for about a week.

TRACEY: Oh, I'm (f) .... to hear that. But you're better now.

MARLENE: Yes, more or less. But it didn't help that my father had just (g) .... his leg.

TRACEY: How did he do that?

MARLENE: He fell when he was (h) .... football with my little brother.

TRACEY: Is his leg in plaster now?

MARLENE: Yes, and he complains all the time. Honestly!

TRACEY: Typical man.

MARLENE: Yes. Anyway, what (i) .... you? How are you, I mean really.

TRACEY: Oh, I'm fine. I wasn't feeling very (j) .... either for a couple of days, but now that I'm back here I feel absolutely great.

MARLENE: Great. So tonight (k) .... go to the beginning-of-term party at the Students' Union!

TRACEY: Brilliant idea!

C Check out

1 Look at the following word map. Extend it by adding more balloons and more words. See how far you can extend it.

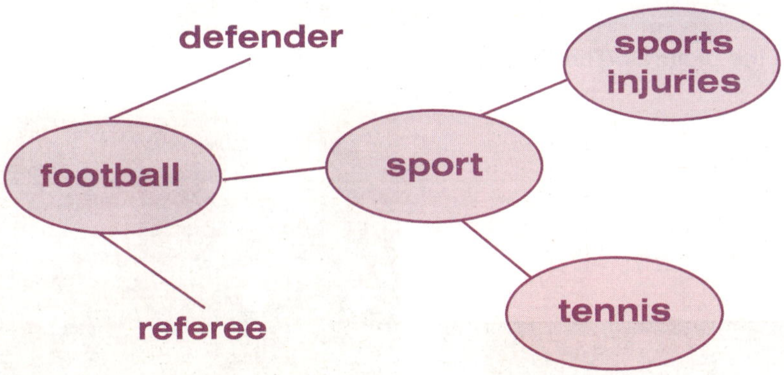

Word list

ankle arm back big toe
break cold collar bone ear
elbow eye flu food poisoning
foot fractured hand head
heel ill index finger injury
knee leg little finger/toe
migraine neck nose
not very well off-colour pain
shoulder sick sore sprained
stiff stomach ache swollen
thigh throat thumb tooth
torso waist wrist

Pronunciation

2 Which is the odd one out in the following groups?

a flu rule toe tooth two
b broken cold swollen throat tooth

Listen to Track 59 and check.

3 Try to make a new word from the following words by changing only one sound. The first one has been done for you.

a ankle ......uncle......
b thumb ....
c pain ....
d hand ....
e nose ....
f wrist ....
g sore ....

4 Listen to Track 60. Tick the words or phrases you hear.

a shoulder [ ]
soldier [ ]
b toys [ ]
toes [ ]
c I'd give him a ring [ ]
I'd give it to him [ ]
d If you ran home [ ]
If you rang home [ ]
e free tickets [ ]
three tickets [ ]

Listen to Track 60 again and repeat what the speakers say.

UNIT 13

A Hobbies and professions

1 Match the words with the numbers in the pictures. The first one is done for you.

a bass guitar	[6]	g piano	[ ]
b cello	[ ]	h saxophone	[ ]
c double bass	[ ]	i trombone	[ ]
d drums	[ ]	j trumpet	[ ]
e guitar	[ ]	k violin	[ ]
f keyboard	[ ]		

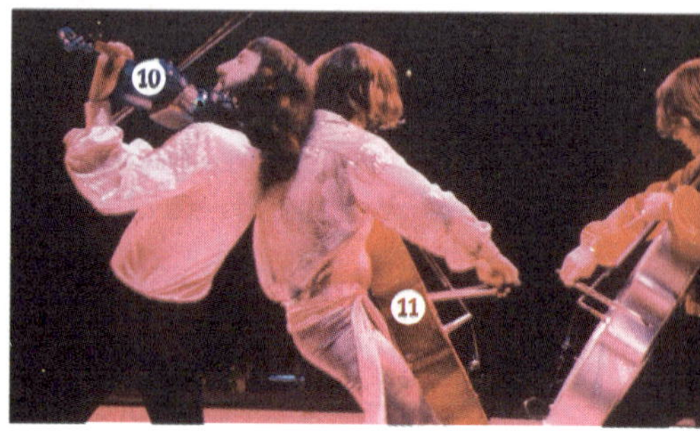

2 Look at the way we make words to describe what people do by using suffixes or adding words, and then do Exercise 3.

WORDS FOR PROFESSIONS AND ACTIVITIES

1 To make words that describe what people do, we often add the *suffix* '-ist' to the *noun*:
*guitar→**guitarist*** *cello→**cellist*** *bass→**bassist*** *science→**scientist***
But after a verb that describes the activity we add the suffix '*-er*', or sometimes '*-or*':
*run→**runner*** *act→**actor*** *drum→**drummer***

2 People who play sports or games are often called ***players***:
*tennis→tennis **player*** *badminton→badminton **player***
Musicians can also be called ***players***, especially if the instrument they play has two or more syllables:
*keyboard→keyboard **player*** *harpsichord→harpsichord **player***

3 Some important exceptions are:
*football→**footballer*** *athletics→**athlete*** *mathematics→**mathematician*** *cooking→**cook***
*yacht→**yachtsman***

3 Can you write the word for someone who:

a ... composes music? ....

b ... manages a band? ....

c ... sings? ....

d ... plays the cello? ....

e ... plays football? ....

f ... plays chess? ....

g ... takes photographs? ....

h ... teaches? ....

i ... works at reception in a hotel? ....

Pronunciation: stressed syllables

4 Underline the stressed syllable in each of the following words.

a mathematics
b photograph
c piano
d saxophone
e biology
f therapy
g trombone
h violin
i reception
j journal

5 Listen to the words on Track 61 and copy them down here. Underline the stressed syllable. Notice how sometimes the stress is different from the related word in Exercise 4. Is the *Same* syllable (S) or a *Different* syllable (D) stressed? The first one is done for you.

a mathematician – D
b ....
c ....
d ....
e ....
f ....
g ....
h ....
i ....
j ....

6 Use some of the words from Exercises 2–5 to identify the occupations in the pictures.

a ....
b ....
c ....
d ....
e ....
f ....
g ....
h ....
i ....
j ....
k ....

B Showing concern

1 Put the following lines of a conversation in the right order. The first one is done for you.

[1] How was the exam?
[ ] You didn't have to do it!
[ ] It was terrible.
[ ] Oh, come on! I'm sure it wasn't that bad.
[ ] Why? What happened?
[ ] I couldn't answer one of the questions. I made a real mess of it.

Now listen to Track 62. Were you correct?

2 Put the expressions in the right place (a–i) on the scale. The first one has been done for you.

- Absolutely terrible.
- It was great.
- I couldn't think what to say/write.
- It wasn't too bad.
- I think it went OK.
- It could have been worse.
- Horrible.
- It went really well.
- I made a real mess of it.

100% (very good)

a ....
b ....
c ....
d ....
e ....
f ....
g ....
h ....
i Absolutely terrible.

0% (very bad)

3 Are the following sentences responding to *Good News* (GN) or *Bad News* (BN)?

a I bet you did all right, really. [ ]
b I'm really pleased to hear it. [ ]
c I'm sure it wasn't as bad as all that. [ ]
d I'm sure it wasn't as bad as you think it was. [ ]
e It can't have been that bad. [ ]
f Oh, you poor thing. [ ]
g Oh good. [ ]
h That's great. [ ]
i That sounds terrible. [ ]

4 **Put the following lines in the correct places in the conversations below.**

1 I don't think I've got the part.
2 I'm really pleased to hear it.
3 I'm sure it wasn't as bad as you think it was.
4 You might have done. There aren't that many good musicians around.
5 It could have been worse.
6 I'm sure I didn't get in.
7 So you think you might have passed?
8 It went brilliantly!

MARK: How was the audition?

JESSY: It was absolutely terrible.
(a) ....

MARK: (b) ....

RACHEL: How was the interview?

SARAH : (c) ....
I think I got the job.

RACHEL: (d) ....

CAROL: How was the exam?

JIM: (e) ....

CAROL: (f) ....

PETER: How was the audition?

JAMES: Horrible (g) ....
They're going to let me know.

PETER: (h) ....

C Check out

1 Which of the words and expressions in the word list do you think will be most useful for you in the future? Why? Which do you think will be the least useful?

Word list

accompanist actor athlete audition badminton bass guitar cello composer conductor double bass drums exam flute guitar harpsichord interview instrument it could have been worse it wasn't too bad keyboard manager mathematician oral exam percussion photographer piano receptionist saxophone singer songwriter sports trial therapist to make a real mess of something trombone trumpet writer violin yachtsman

Pronunciation

2 What common sound do the words in each group below (a–c) share: /aɪ/ like *light*, /iː/ like *see*, or /ɪ/ like *sit*?

a audition, badminton, exam, guitar, trumpet, violin: ……………………

……………………

b athlete, keyboard, pianist: ……………………

……………………

c might, right, trial, violin, writer: ……………………

……………………

Listen to Track 63 to check your answers.

Write some other words you know that have the same sounds as those above. Look at the different ways the sounds are spelt.

d /ɪ/: ……………………

e /iː/: ……………………

f /aɪ/: ……………………

3 Look at the following words and mark the stress patterns.

a receptionist b percussion c saxophone d violin

Listen to Track 64 to check.

4 Listen to Track 65. Write the words you hear in the correct column of the table. The first one is done for you.

a Ooo	b oOo	c ooO	d oOoo
audience			

Write two more words that you can think of that have the same stress pattern in each column in the table.

AUDIOSCRIPT

Track 1

JANE: Come on, Polly, there's someone I'd like you to meet.
POLLY: Oh, all right.
JANE: Andy, this is Polly. She's in advertising too.
ANDY: Oh, hi. Nice to meet you.
POLLY: Yeah, nice to meet you too.
ANDY: What do you do in advertising?
POLLY: Not much really.
ANDY: Sorry?
POLLY: Oh, I mean I only started last week. It's my first job. What about you?
ANDY: Me? Oh well, I'm working on a TV commercial for an Internet bank at the moment.
POLLY: That sounds interesting.
ANDY: Yes, yes it is.

Track 2

all, arm, door, seem, smell, stare, ought, walk, work, store, out, saw

Track 3

The three-syllable words are: *assertive, confident, decisive, designer, firefighter, footballer, impatient, journalist, orchestral conductor, organised, personal assistant, primary, collector, romantic, salary, sensitive*
The four-syllable words are: *conscientious, considerate, emotional, hospitable, intelligent, interesting, occupation, sympathetic*

Track 4

'c' is pronounced in two ways: as /k/ in *confident, conscientious, considerate, doctor, enthusiastic, occupation, orchestral, conductor, collector, romantic, sympathetic*; and as /s/ in *decisive* and *sincere*

Track 5

a What do you think of Lisa?
b What do you do in advertising?
c Have you two met before?
d How long have you known Ruth?
e Can I ask you a question?
f Do you enjoy studying zoology?
g What time is your taxi coming?

Track 6

REPORTER: What did you think of that rollercoaster ride?
YOUNG LAD: It was pretty frightening.
REPORTER: What about you sir?
MAN: It was absolutely terrifying.
REPORTER: Did you enjoy it?
SCHOOLGIRL: Yeah. It was quite good.
GRANNY: Oh, come now, dear. It wasn't just 'quite good', it was absolutely fantastic!

Track 7

MAN 1: Have you ever seen the original film of *Psycho*?
MAN 2: Yes.
MAN 1: What did you think of it?
MAN 2: It was absolutely terrifying.
MAN 3: (Do) you really think so?
MAN 2: Why? Didn't you?
MAN 3: No, not really. It's not my kind of film. I thought it was rather boring.

Track 8

I like playing games in my head.
Absolutely fascinating.
The film was amazing.
It was rather boring when I saw it, I remember.
I went to all his films when I was at school.
What happened at the end of the film?
I completely agree.
It makes me very angry.
Call me when you've seen the film.
Have you seen any films recently?
I haven't read that book.

Track 9

absolutely, amazing, angry, bad, fairly, fantastic, fascinating, hilarious, rather, really

Track 10

a He's rather interesting.
b I was pretty scared.
c It was absolutely amazing.
d It was absolutely hilarious.
e She was rather angry.
f They're really good.
g Your room's absolutely filthy.

Track 11

a I've still got some last-minute shopping to do before the party tomorrow.
b I don't really need to buy anything. I'm just window-shopping to see what the new fashions are like.
c I prefer to do all my shopping at a shopping centre because everything you need is there, and there's usually somewhere to have a coffee when you've finished.
d How do you fancy a really good shopping expedition? We could stay in town for the whole day.
e I don't agree with Sunday shopping. We should have one day when everyone can relax.
f Excuse me sir, where did you get this shopping trolley?

Track 12

ASSISTANT: Can I help you?
CUSTOMER: No thanks. I'm just looking around.
ASSISTANT: OK. Let me know if I can help you with anything.
CUSTOMER: Thanks.
ASSISTANT: No problem.

CUSTOMER: Excuse me.
ASSISTANT: Yes. How can I help you?
CUSTOMER: I'm looking for Takez jeans.
ASSISTANT: I'm afraid we don't sell Takez.
CUSTOMER: Oh, that's a pity. Do you know where I could find some?
ASSISTANT: Well, you could try the shop on the corner. They might be able to help.
CUSTOMER: Thanks.
ASSISTANT: You're welcome.

CUSTOMER: Excuse me. Do you have any belts?
ASSISTANT: Yes we do. They're over there by those shirts.
CUSTOMER: Oh yes, so they are. Thanks.

Track 13

The words with the same sounds are:

- /e/ in *anything, belt, dress, every, help, many, several, sweater, welcome*
- /æ/ in *cap, hat*
- /iː/ in *fleece, jeans, please*
- /ʌ/ in *gloves, much, some*
- /ɜː/ in *shirt, skirt, T-shirt*

Track 14

cap	hat
hat	sandals
belt	sweater
sweater	centre
Sunday	gloves
fleece	jeans
minute	list
shirt	skirt
shopping	socks
mall	shorts

Track 15

shirt, shorts, T-shirt

Track 16

a There's a nice stall in the market.
There're nice stalls in the market.
b Very few people eat meat.
Very few people eat meat.
c I'll do the late-night shopping on Friday.
I do the late-night shopping on Friday.
d It makes me feel angry.
It makes me feel hungry.
e Can I help you?
Can I help you?
f I'm looking for a fleece.
I'm looking for the police.

Track 17

TRAVEL AGENT: Yes, can I help you?
BEN: We'd like to book a holiday.
DUNCAN: Yes, can you recommend anything?
TRAVEL AGENT: Well, what kind of holiday do you want?
DUNCAN: Oh you know, sun, sea, sand, the usual.
TRAVEL AGENT: OK, what about somewhere in Spain, say Sitges near Barcelona?
BEN: Well, we've been to Spain once already.
TRAVEL AGENT: Well then, how about Sorrento in Italy?
DUNCAN: Italy? That's a great idea, but actually we'd prefer somewhere a bit more, well, exotic.
TRAVEL AGENT: All right then, can I suggest Rio de Janeiro?
BEN: I don't think we could afford that.
TRAVEL AGENT: Actually, it's probably not as expensive as you think.
DUNCAN: Yes, but is it worth it?
TRAVEL AGENT: Well, it's definitely worth considering.
BEN: Can I have a look at the brochure?
TRAVEL AGENT: Sure. Take your time.
BEN: Thanks.

Track 18

a That sounds fantastic.
b That sounds like a great idea.
c That's exactly what I want.
d That's just right.
e That's incredible.
f That's a great suggestion.

Track 19

backpacking, camping, campsite, gallery, track, package

Track 20

1 *package, vacation, backpacking, camping, fantastic* – *vacation* is the odd one out.
2 *clubbing, cruise, public, sunbathe, fun* – *cruise* is the odd one out.
3 *backpacking, boating, excursion, holiday, waterski* – *boating* is the odd one out.
4 *camping, culture, hotel, museum, sunbathe* – *museum* is the odd one out.
5 *gallery, nightlife, sunbathe, resort, swimming* – *resort* is the odd one out.
6 *holiday, gallery, excursion, sightseeing, luxury* – *excursion* is the odd one out.

Track 21

a That ship is really big.
b Phew! It's very hot in here.
c I don't like the noise that sheep make.
d This is a nice place.
e It's a really good club.
f After two weeks on holiday I feel fat.
g The weather's better this week, isn't it?
h What's the plan for tomorrow?
i I always choose holidays in the sun.
j Excuse me, that's my seat.

Track 22

WOMAN: Matt! Kate! How nice to see you.
MATT: Yes. It's great to be here.
MAN: Can I take your coats?
KATE: Thank you.

Track 23

Can I get you something to drink?
Can I take your coat?
Did you have any trouble finding us?
Do you need to freshen up?
Do you want to wash your hands?
Go on into the sitting room.
How nice to see you.
Thanks for coming.

Track 24

Yes please. I'd like an orange juice.
No. It was quite straightforward, actually.
Thank you.
Thank you. Is it through here?
Yes, that would be nice. Where's the bathroom?
Well, thanks for inviting us.
Yes. It's great to be here.

Track 25

bungalow, cold, cope, go, homeless, mobile home, studio

Track 26

homecoming, home-made, homesick, homework, houseboat

Track 27

block, cramped, ground, spacious

Track 28

a It's great to see you.
b Oh, this is great!
c Can I take your coat?
d It's a bit cramped in here.
e I've just won a prize.
f Can I get you something to drink?
g Thanks for inviting us.

Track 29

a

HELEN: That's a really nice jacket.
SAM: Oh, thanks.
HELEN: Where did you get it?
SAM: From that shop opposite the bank.
HELEN: Oh yes. I know the one. Well, it really suits you.
SAM: Thanks.

b

JASON: I like your shirt.
LEO: Do you?
JASON: Yes.
LEO: It was a present from my girlfriend.
JASON: Well, it looks good on you. What's it made of?
LEO: I don't know. Cotton, I think.

c

SUNITA: Those are really nice earrings.
KAREN: I'm glad you like them.
SUNITA: Where did you get them?
KAREN: I was given them by my aunt. They're from Japan, I think.
SUNITA: Well, I think they're great.

Track 30

WOMAN: I've just passed my driving test.
MAN: That's fantastic.
WOMAN: I earn my living as a writer.
MAN: How interesting!
WOMAN: I study chemistry.
MAN: That is interesting.
WOMAN: I love dance music.
MAN: Oh, really?
WOMAN: I'm thinking of getting married.
MAN: You're thinking of getting married?
WOMAN: I live in Birmingham.
MAN: You live in Birmingham?

Track 31

In most of the words the first syllable is stressed: *capture, conquer, corduroy, cotton, denim, educate, execute, guilty, leather, marry, nylon, pirate, plastic, poison, prison, sentence, soldier*
In these words the second syllable is stressed: *accuse, defeat, disguise, divorced, elect, escape, imprison, inherit*
In this word the third syllable is stressed: *polyester*

Track 32

The words with the sound /ɔː/ are: *worn, born, corduroy, divorced*
The words with the sound /ɒ/ are: *song, conquer, cotton, nylon, polyester*
The words with the sound /ɔɪ/ are: *corduroy, poison*
The words with the sound /ə/ are: *photograph, cotton, imprison, poison, prison*
The words with the sound /əʊ/ are: *oh, soldier*
The words with the sound / uː/ are: *pool, shoot*
Wool doesn't fit any of the boxes.

Track 33

1

VICAR: Repeat after me. I, Mary Ann Calhoun …
MARY: I, Mary Ann Calhoun …
VICAR: … take thee, Robin James Archibald …
MARY: … take thee, Robin James Archibald …
VICAR: … to be my lawful wedded husband …
MARY: … to be my lawful wedded husband …
VICAR: … to have and to hold from this day forth …
MARY: … to have and to hold from this day forth …
VICAR: … for better or worse …
MARY: … for better or worse …
VICAR: … for richer or poorer …
MARY: … for richer or poorer …
VICAR: … forsaking all others till death us do part …
MARY: … forsaking all others till death us do part …
VICAR: … and hereto I plight thee my troth.
MARY: … and hereto I plight thee my troth.

2

MAN: Do you want to marry her?
GERMAN MAN: Why yes, I surely do.
MAN: What about you?
GERMAN WOMAN: Oh, yeah. Me too.
MAN: OK. That's it. How about a kiss?

3

REGISTRAR: Do you, Kazuo Otami, agree to marry this woman?
KAZUO: Yes, I do.
REGISTRAR: Do you, Muriel Spallsworthy, agree to marry this man?
MURIEL: Yes, I do. Sure thing.
REGISTRAR: Then by the power invested in me by the state of Queensland, I declare that you are legally married. You may kiss the bride.
KAZUO: You bet!

4

FACILITATOR: I understand that you have both written your own wedding contracts. Is that correct?
BEN: Yes. I, Ben Finkelburn, promise to love you forever. I agree to do the washing and almost all the ironing. I promise to do half the cooking and I'll do the gardening at least three times a year. And I give you my word that I won't wear my yellow suit again or play my saxophone more than twice a week.
FACILITATOR: And now you, Mariah.
MARIAH: Yes. Right. Well, I promise to love you forever, I guess. And I promise to cook half the time, and I agree to let you drive my car on Sundays. And I give you my word that you can watch sport on TV from eight to nine most nights. I promise to pretend that it's interesting.
FACILITATOR: Right. Is that all?
MARIAH: Yes.
BEN: Yes.
FACILITATOR: OK then. I guess this means you're married.
ONLOOKER: Wow!

Track 34

I will do it tomorrow.
I'll do it tomorrow.
I will have that coffee now, please.
I'll have that coffee now, please.
I will answer the telephone.
I'll answer the telephone.
I will talk to you later.
I'll talk to you later.
I will be home at nine.
I'll be home at nine.
I will never forget this.
I'll never forget this.

Track 35

The words that sound like *day,* are *break*, *away*, *make*, *take*.
The words that sound like *cow*, are *out*, *down*, *round*, *about*.
The word that sounds like *so,* is *go*.

Track 36

a I **promise** I'll be at your house by four o'clock.
b I promise I'll be at your house by **four o'clock**.
c I promise I'll be at your **house** by four o'clock.
d I promise **I'll** be at your house by four o'clock.
e I promise I'll be at **your** house by four o'clock.

Track 37

a advertisement, advertisement
b brochure, brochure
c cinema, cinema
d controversy, controversy
e entertainer, entertainer
f interesting, interesting
g lieutenant, lieutenant
h officer, officer
i opinion, opinion
j simultaneous, simultaneous

Track 38

a Can I sit here, please?
Yes, certainly.
b Can I use my camera in here?
No, sir. I'm afraid taking photographs is strictly forbidden.
c Are dogs allowed in here?
No, sorry. We operate a 'no dogs' policy.
d Is it OK if I use my mobile phone in here?
I'd rather you didn't.
e Is it all right if I take one of these?
Sure. Help yourself.
f Do you mind if I bring my sister to the party?
Not at all. We'd love to meet her.

Track 39

The word with the sound like *fine* is *library*.
The word with the sound like *liar* is *bonfire*.
The word with the sound like *fear* is *here*.

Track 40

amazing, certainly, exactly, forbidden, graffiti, occasion, opinion, permission, sensitive, signature

Track 41

different, interest, usually, consciously, general, intimacy, subconsciously, relaxation

Track 42

a

ACTOR: How do I play this scene?
DIRECTOR: It's difficult to say. I think you're probably quite angry in this bit.
ACTOR: OK, so what do you recommend?
DIRECTOR: I think you can come in and shake your fist at Caspar as you start talking.
ACTOR: Anything else?

DIRECTOR: Well, you could fold your arms then so that you go on looking angry.
ACTOR: Is this what you had in mind?
DIRECTOR: Yes, that's the type of thing.

b

ACTOR: How do you want me to do this scene?
DIRECTOR: That's not easy to say. My impression is that you're probably a bit bored in this scene.
ACTOR: OK. So what do I do?
DIRECTOR: Well, I think you can show boredom by folding your arms, or crossing your legs when you sit down.
ACTOR: Is that all?
DIRECTOR: Well, you could shrug your shoulders when she talks to you.
ACTOR: Like this?
DIRECTOR: Yes, that's the kind of thing.

Track 43

cross, finger, indifference, puzzled, strangers, truth

Track 44

intimacy, relaxation, subconsciously

Track 45

1 Stop biting your nails!
2 I'm pleased to see you.
3 Don't shake your fist at me!
4 I am telling the truth.
5 It's so nice to see you.
6 Are you waving at me?
7 Don't raise your eyebrows at me!
8 I quite agree with you.
9 I can't be absolutely sure.

Track 46

a

RON: Computer Helpline, Ron speaking.
KARL: Oh, hello. Can you help me?
RON: What's the problem?
KARL: Well, I can't get my personal organiser to work with my computer.
RON: OK. Have you checked the batteries in your organiser?
KARL: Yes, of course.
RON: Have you checked the connection at the back of your computer?
KARL: No. Do you think that will help?
RON: Do I think it will help? Well, why don't you try and see?

b

RACHEL: Hello. Computer Helpline. Rachel speaking. What seems to be the problem?
JIM: Umm, well I know this is silly, but do you know how to connect up to the Internet?
RACHEL: What system are you using?
JIM: It's an Apple Mac.
RACHEL: OK. Do you have an Internet icon on your screen? Like a globe?
JIM: Yes. Yes, I do.
RACHEL: Well then, just click on the icon and you're away.
JIM: OK ... oh, yes. Thanks. That's great!
RACHEL: You're welcome.

c

MIKE: Hi, Computer Helpline. My name's Mike. How may I help you?
JANE: This thing is driving me crazy!
MIKE: Hold on! What's the problem?
JANE: Well, my computer seems to have crashed.
MIKE: How exactly?
JANE: Well, I can't move anything. Even the cursor just sticks in the same place.
MIKE: OK, well the best thing to do is to switch off and start again.
JANE: Really?
MIKE: Yes, really. That's what I would do.
JANE: OK. I'll give it a try. Thanks.
MIKE: No problem.

Track 47

Can you help me? (x 2)
What seems to be the problem? (x 2)
Have you checked the batteries? (x 2)
Do you know how to use this answerphone? (x 2)
What is the problem? (x 2)
What do I do now? (x 2)

Track 48

The words for column 1 are: *electric, computer.*
The words for column 2 are: *personal, microwave, monitor, stereo.*
The words for column 3 are: *television, electronic.*
The words for column 4 are: *organiser, calculator.*

Track 49

The words for column 1 are: *credit, microwave, crashed.*
The words for column 2 are: *disk, scanner.*
The words for column 3 are: *electric, electronic.*

Track 50

a Thank you.
b Thank you.
c Thanks a lot.
d Thank you very much.
e Thank you very much for your help.
f No problem.
g Don't mention it.
h Glad I could help.

Track 51

NANCY: How was the film?
JIM: It was a disaster. Halfway through they stopped it and told us we had to leave.
NANCY: You must have been really fed up.
JIM: Well, yes. We all had to go out into the street, even though it was raining.
NANCY: That can't have been much fun.
JIM: No, it certainly wasn't. I got soaked. But then, when we were allowed back, they started the film again and offered all of us free tickets to any film for the next month.
NANCY: You must have been pleased.
JIM: I certainly was. Would you like to come to the next film with me?

Track 52

a

MAN: How was the film?
WOMAN: Fantastic.
MAN: Fantastic?
WOMAN: Fantastic!

b

WOMAN: How long do you think the film was?
MAN: An hour and a half?
WOMAN: Ha!
MAN: Two hours?
WOMAN: Ha!
MAN: Two and a half hours?
WOMAN: Keep going.
MAN: Three hours??
WOMAN: Three and a half hours.
MAN: Three and a half hours??!
WOMAN: Yes.
MAN: No!!
WOMAN: Yes. Three and a half hours.
MAN: Three and a half hours!!

Track 53

The letter 'g' can be pronounced /g/: *autobiography, biography.*
The letter 'g' can also be pronounced /dʒ/: *logical, tragedy.*

Track 54

Autobiography has six syllables.
Animated and *biography* have four syllables.

Track 55

a You might have hurt yourself.
b You can't have been very pleased.
c That must have been terrifying.
d You could have been in real danger.
e That couldn't have been pleasant.

Track 56

Here are today's football scores:
Everton 0, Sunderland ...
Aston Villa 2, Sheffield United ...
Liverpool 1, Burnley ...
Newcastle United 2, Manchester United ...
Blackburn Rovers 0, Sheffield Wednesday ...
Arsenal 2, Manchester City ...
Tottenham Hotspur 3, Leeds United ...

Track 57

Here are today's football scores:
Everton 0, Sunderland 1.
Aston Villa 2, Sheffield United 2.
Liverpool 1, Burnley 3.
Newcastle United 2, Manchester United 3.
Blackburn Rovers 0, Sheffield Wednesday 0.
Arsenal 2, Manchester City 1.
Tottenham Hotspur 3, Leeds United 2.

Track 58

VICKY: Hi Jane, how are you?
JANE: I'm fine. How about you?
VICKY: Oh, fine, I suppose. You're looking well, by the way.
JANE: Thanks. I had an infection. I was off work, but I'm better now.
VICKY: Good.
JANE: But what about you? You look terrible.
VICKY: Thanks!
JANE: No sorry, I mean ...
VICKY: It's all right. It's true; I have been a bit under the weather, recently ... work, that kind of thing.
JANE: Oh, poor you. Listen, why not come round after the practice and I'll try and cheer you up.
VICKY: Oh, I don't really think I'm up to it. Do you mind?
JANE: No, not at all. Get well soon.

Track 59

a *flu, rule, toe, tooth, two* – *toe* is the odd one out.
b *broken, cold, swollen, throat, tooth* – *tooth* is the odd one out.

Track 60

a Ow! My shoulder hurts.
b Look at his toes! They're broken.
c If I was you, I'd give it to him.
d If you rang home now, it would be all right.
e If you do this work for me, I'll give you three tickets.

Track 61

a mathematician
b photographer
c pianist
d saxophonist
e biologist
f therapist
g trombonist
h violinist
i receptionist
j journalist

Track 62

STUDENT 1: How was the exam?
STUDENT 2: It was terrible.
STUDENT 1: Why? What happened?
STUDENT 2: I couldn't answer one of the questions. I made a real mess of it.
STUDENT 1: Oh come on! I'm sure it wasn't that bad.
STUDENT 2: You didn't have to do it!

Track 63

a *audition, badminton, exam, guitar, trumpet*, and *violin* have the sound /ɪ/ like the word *sit*.
b *athlete, keyboard* and *pianist* have the sound /iː/ like the word *see*.
c *might, right, trial, violin* and *writer* have the sound /aɪ/ like *light*.

Track 64

a receptionist
b percussion
c saxophone
d violin

Track 65

audience, conductor, engineer, interview, manager, photographer, remember, songwriter, therapist

ANSWER KEY

UNIT 1

A 1

a footballer
b nurse
c designer
d primary teacher
e orchestral conductor
f soldier
g personal assistant
h refuse collector
i journalist
j firefighter

A 4

Example answers

a A footballer should be assertive, confident and decisive.
b A nurse should be friendly, kind and sympathetic.
c A designer should be confident, intelligent and sincere.
d A primary teacher should be considerate, enthusiastic and interesting.
e An orchestral conductor should be assertive, confident and enthusiastic.
f A soldier should be assertive, decisive and loyal.
g A personal assistant should be decisive, honest and loyal.
h A refuse collector should be considerate, happy and patient.
i A journalist should be considerate, intelligent and interesting.
j A firefighter should be confident, considerate and decisive.

A 5

a assertive: behaving in a confident way in which you are quick to express your opinions and feelings

sensitive: showing that you care about someone or something and do not want to cause offence

b assertive: You need to be more assertive to succeed in business.

sensitive: This is a difficult case which needs sensitive and skilful handling.

A 6

un-: unassertive, unconfident, unemotional, unenthusiastic, unfriendly, unhappy, unintelligent, uninteresting, unkind, unpleasant, unromantic, unsympathetic

in-: inconsiderate, indecisive, inhospitable, insensitive, insincere

im-: impatient

dis-: dishonest, disloyal

A 7

a indecisive
b honest
c inhospitable
d dishonest
e Sympathetic
f impatient
g unkind
h unromantic
i enthusiastic
j sensitive
k loyal

B 1

a Oh, all right.
b Yeah, nice to meet you too.
c Not much really.
d Oh, I mean I only started last week. It's my first job. What about you?
e That sounds interesting.

B 2

a There's someone I'd like you to meet.
b Andy, this is Polly.
c I'd like you to meet Andy.
d Polly's in advertising.
e Nice to meet you.
f Are you a friend of Polly's?
g Do you like what you do?
h How do you know our host?
i What are you working on at the moment?
j What do you do?
k Oh really?
l That sounds interesting.
m What a coincidence! I'm an actor too.

B 3

a There's someone I'd like you to meet.
b I think you'll like him.
c Yeah, nice to meet you too.
d Do you enjoy studying zoology?
e I'm a teacher.
f That's a coincidence.
g Can I ask you a question?
h Aren't you a bit young to be a teacher?

B 4

The words all share the sound /ɔː/ like *call*.

B 5

all, door, ought, walk, store, saw

C 2

a designer, doctor, firefighter, footballer, journalist, nurse, orchestral conductor personal assistant (PA), primary teacher, refuse collector, soldier
b assertive, confident, conscientious, considerate, decisive, emotional, enthusiastic, friendly, happy, honest, hospitable, impatient, intelligent, interesting, kind, loyal, organised, patient, pleasant, romantic, sensitive, sincere, sympathetic

C 3

a three-syllable words: assertive, confident, decisive, designer, firefighter, footballer, impatient, journalist, orchestral conductor, organised, personal assistant, primary, collector, romantic, salary, sensitive

four-syllable words: conscientious, considerate, emotional, hospitable, intelligent, interesting, occupation, sympathetic

b 'c' is pronounced in two ways: as /k/ in *confident, conscientious, considerate, doctor, enthusiastic, occupation, orchestral, conductor, collector, romantic, sympathetic*; and as /s/ in *decisive* and *sincere.*

C 4

a down
b up
c up
d down
e up
f up
g up

UNIT 2

A 1

angry – furious, bad – terrible, big – enormous, cold – freezing, dirty – filthy, frightening – terrifying, funny – hilarious, good – fantastic, hot – boiling, interesting – fascinating, surprising – amazing

A 2

a frightening
b terrifying
c good
d fantastic

A 3

The four combinations that are not possible are: b, f, h, i

A 4

a *Absolute* is an adjective. *Absolutely* is an adverb.
b *Absolute* is followed by a noun. *Absolutely* is followed by (1) an adjective, (2) a verb like *hate.*
c We use *absolutely not* in speech.

A 5

a absolutely enormous!
b absolutely/really furious!
c absolutely/really/completely terrible!
d absolutely/really/completely fantastic!

e absolutely/really filthy!
f absolutely/really boiling!
g absolutely/really/completely terrifying!
h absolutely/really freezing!
(Note: we tend to use *completely* only when we are talking about things and not about people.)

B 1

The missing lines are:
What did you think of it?
Why? Didn't you?

B 2

a Have you ever....?
b What did you think of it?
c It was ......

B 3

a D
b A
c A
d D
e D
f A
g A

B 4

a television
b saw
c ago
d before
e think
f Do
g agree
h thought
i Really
j knew
k in
l didn't
m thought
n too
o two
p film
q last
r going
s Probably
t film
u fantastic
v agree
w immediately
x is
y will
z absolutely/quite

B 5

a absolutely, fascinating, happened, angry, at
b saw, all, call
c amazing, was, agree
d any, read
e playing, games, fascinating, amazing, makes

C 2

c absolutely, amazing, angry, bad, fairly, fantastic, fascinating, hilarious, rather, really

C 3

a He's rather interesting.
b I was pretty scared.
c It was absolutely amazing.
d It was absolutely hilarious.
e She was rather angry.
f They're really good.
g Your room's absolutely filthy!

UNIT 3

A 1

a uncountable
b because it says [U]
c American English

A 2

a shopping trolley, shopping centre, shopping complex, shopping expedition, shopping bag, shopping list, shopping malls
b do the shopping, go shopping, Internet shopping, last-minute shopping, late-night shopping, serious shopping, Sunday shopping, window-shopping

A 3

a last-minute shopping
b window-shopping
c shopping centre
d shopping expedition
e Sunday shopping
f shopping trolley

A 4

a shopping expedition
b last-minute shopping
c late-night shopping
d window-shopping
e shopping
f shopping trolley
g do the shopping
h Internet shopping

B 1

a 4
b 1
c 2
d 3

B 3

The words with the same sounds are: /e/ in *anything, belt, dress, every, help, many, several, sweater, welcome*; /æ/ in *cap, hat*; /iː/ in *fleece, jeans, please*; /ʌ/ in *gloves, much, some*; /ɜː/ in *shirt, skirt, T-shirt.*

B 4

a Barbara: a dress, a sweater, boots and a hat
b Charlene: sandals, shorts, a T-shirt, a belt and a cap
c Donald: trousers, a shirt, a sweater and a hat
d Phoebe: a skirt, a T-shirt, a belt and socks
e Margaret: a dress, some tights, a hat and gloves
f Ashley: jeans, a shirt, a fleece and a cap

B 5

a 2
b 5
c 1
d 3
e 4
f 7
g 6
h 8

C 1

There are two meaning groups.

Clothes: belt, cap, fleece, gloves, hat, jeans, sandals, shirt, shorts, skirt, socks, sweater, tights, trousers, T-shirt

Shopping vocabulary: last-minute shopping, late-night shopping, serious shopping, shopping bag, shopping centre, shopping complex, shopping list, shopping mall, shopping spree, shopping trolley, Sunday shopping, to do the shopping, to go shopping, window-shopping

C 2

a cap – hat, hat – sandals, belt – sweater, sweater – centre, Sunday – gloves, fleece – jeans, minute – list, shirt – skirt, shopping – socks, mall – shorts
b shorts, shirt, T-shirt

C 3

a D
b S
c D
d D
e S
f D

UNIT 4

A 1

a 5
b 3
c 1
d 6
e 2
f 4

A 2

a backpacking, boating, campsite, pony-trekking, surfing, waterski, swimming
b boating, campsite, excellent facilities, swimming pool, swimming
c culture, excellent facilities, excursion, luxury, vacation
d hotel, nightlife, sunbathing, swimming pool, resort, clubbing, surfing, tourist, waterski
e museums, galleries, culture, excursion, hotel, vacation

A 3

a *vacation* (American English), *holiday* (British English) – we know because they both have entries that say 'n' (= noun) and 'v' (=verb).
b *vacation* – that's what it says in the definition.
c British English speakers use the word *holidaymaker*. American English speakers use the word *vacationer*.

A 4
a cruise
b interesting
c museum
d sunbathing
e tourists
f air-conditioned
g package holiday

A 5
The word is *campsite*.

A 6
a abroad
b backpacking
c excursion
d gallery
e holidaymaker
f resort
g sightseeing
h vacation

B 1
a Yes, can I help you?
b Well, what kind of holiday do you want?
c OK, what about somewhere in Spain, say Sitges near Barcelona?
d Well then, how about Sorrento in Italy?
e All right then, can I suggest Rio de Janeiro
f Actually, it's probably not as expensive as you think.
g Well, it's definitely worth considering.
h Sure. Take your time.

B 3
a enthusiastic
b enthusiastic
c unenthusiastic
d enthusiastic
e unenthusiastic
f unenthusiastic

C 2
a backpacking, camping, campsite, gallery, track, package
b 1 *vacation* is the odd one out.
2 *cruise* is the odd one out.
3 *boating* is the odd one out.
4 *museum* is the odd one out.
5 *resort* is the odd one out.
6 *excursion* is the odd one out.

C 3
a big
b hot
c sheep
d nice
e good
f fat
g better
h plan
i choose
j seat

UNIT 5

A 1
bare – cluttered, cold – warm, cramped – spacious, light – dark, untidy – tidy

A 3
a Home-grown
b Homeless
c Home-made
d Homesick
e Homework
f Homecoming

A 4
1 block of flats
2 ground floor
3 first floor
4 flat
5 studio flat
6 bungalow
7 garden
8 semi-detached house
9 garage
10 terraced house
11 basement
12 cottage
13 fence
14 gate

A 5
a It's a noun. (It says 'n'.)
b /gɑːdn/
c yard
d four

B 1
A: Matt! Kate! How nice to see you.
B: Yes. It's great to be here.
C: Can I take your coats?
D: Thank you.

B 2
a Can I get you something to drink?
b Can I take your coat?
c Did you have any trouble finding us?
d Do you want/need to wash your hands/freshen up?
e Go on into the sitting room.
f How nice to see you!
g Thanks for coming.

B 3
a Can I get you something to drink?
b Did you have any trouble finding us?
c Can I take your coat?
d Go on into the sitting room.
e Do you need to freshen up?
f Thanks for coming.
g How nice to see you!

B 4
a Yes please. I'd like an orange juice.
b No. It was quite straightforward, actually.
c Thank you.
d Thank you. Is it through here?
e Yes, that would be nice. Where's the bathroom?
f Well, thanks for inviting us.
g Yes. It's great to be here.

B 6
a Thanks for coming.
b Can I get you something to drink?
c Did you have any trouble finding your way here?
d Can I take your coat?
e Do you need to freshen up?
f How nice to see you.
g We got a bit lost, but it wasn't too bad.
h Yes please. Have you got an orange juice?
i Can you tell me where the bathroom is?
j It's great to see you.
k No, I think I'll keep it on if that's all right.

B 7
a Can I get you something to drink?
b Can I take your coat?
c Did you have any trouble finding your way here?
d Do you need to freshen up?
e How nice to see you.
f It's great to see you.
g No, I think I'll keep it on if that's all right.
h We got a bit lost, but it wasn't too bad.
i Yes please. Have you got an orange juice?
j Can you tell me where the bathroom is?

C 2
Words with a positive feeling: homecoming, home-made, light, spacious, tidy, warm.
Words with a negative feeling: accident, bare, cluttered, cold, cramped, dark, homeless, homesick, untidy

C 3
a The sound is /əʊ/ like *so*.
b homecoming, home-made, homesick, homework, houseboat, studio
c block, cramped, ground, spacious

C 4
a It's great to see you.
b Oh, this is great!
c Can I take your coat?
d It's a bit cramped in here.
e I've just won a prize.
f Can I get you something to drink?
g Thanks for inviting us.

UNIT 6

A 1
a accuse
b guilty
c sentence ... prison
d pirate ... captured ... soldiers
e escaped ... disguised
f conquered ... crowned
g defeated
h elected
i died ... poison
j stabbed
k executed
l shot
m born ... brought up
n educated
o inherited
p married ... divorced

A 2

b **Verb (past participle)**
accused
conquered
crowned
defeated
died
disguised
divorced
educated
elected
escaped
executed
imprisoned
inherited
married
poisoned
sentenced
shot
stabbed

c **Noun**
accusation
conquest
crown
defeat
death
disguise
divorce
education
election
escape
execution
imprisonment
inheritance
marriage
poison
sentence
shooting
stabbing

A 3

a Eight
b It means that *crown* is one of the 3000 most common words in written English.
c [C] means that the noun is countable (we can say *one crown, two crowns, three crowns* etc.). It is not the same as 'usually singular'.

B 1

a From that shop opposite the bank.
b It was a present from my girlfriend.
c I was given them by my aunt.

B 2

Saying you like something: That's a really nice jacket. I like your shirt. Those are really nice earrings. I think they're great.

Saying something is good for the person who is wearing it: Well, it really suits you. It looks good on you.

Being pleased that someone compliments you: Oh, thanks. Thanks. I'm glad you like them.

B 3

a plastic
b leather
c silk
d wool
e corduroy
f denim

B 4

a 1 Oh thanks.
2 It was a present from my husband.
b 1 It was given to me by my aunt.
2 Well, it looks good with that suit. What's it made of?
c 1 Where did you get it?
2 Oh yes. So it's a Swiss watch then?
3 No I don't think so. It's from Korea.

B 5

a That's fantastic.
b How interesting!
c That is interesting.
d Oh, really?
e You're thinking of getting married?
f You live in Birmingham?

C 1

a conquer, elect, escape, inherit, marry
b accuse, defeat, die, divorced, execute, guilty, imprison, pirate, poison, prison, sentence, shoot, stab
c (all the others)

C 2

a Stress on the first syllable: *capture, conquer, corduroy, cotton, denim, educate, execute, guilty, leather, marry, nylon, pirate, plastic, poison, prison, sentence, soldier*

Stress on the second syllable: *accuse, defeat, disguise, divorced, elect, escape, imprison, inherit*

Stress on the third syllable: *polyester*

b /ɔː/: worn, born, corduroy, divorced
/ɒ/: song, conquer, cotton, nylon, polyester
/ɔɪ/: corduroy, poison
/ə/: photograph, cotton, imprison, poison, prison
/əʊ/: oh, soldier
/uː/: pool, shoot
Wool doesn't fit in any of the boxes.

C 3

a capture, crown, defeat, disguise, escape, pirate, poison, sentence
b corduroy, cotton, denim, leather, nylon, plastic, polyester, silk, wool (These are all words that describe materials.)

UNIT 7

A 2

a give away, give back, give out
b give in to, give off

A 3

a Some dictionaries give eight, others give nine.
b cut out, cut up

A 4

a make a go of
b take up
c go on working out
d set up
e get round to
f break up with
g see about
h cut down on
i put in

A 5

a Type 1: work out
b Type 2: take up, set up, put in
c Type 3: go on, see about
d Type 4: break up with, make a go of, get round to, cut down on

A 6

a broke up with
b go on
c make a go of
d set up
e put in
f get round to
g took up
h cut down on
i Give up

B 2

a 4
b 1
c 2
d 3

B 3

Ben
a ... love you forever.
... do half the cooking.
b ... do the washing and almost all the ironing.
c ...do the gardening at least three times a year.
d ... I won't wear my yellow suit again.
... I won't play my saxophone more than twice a week.

Mariah
a ... love you forever.
... cook half the time.
b ... pretend that it's interesting.
... let you drive my car on Sundays.
d ... you can watch sport on TV from 8 to 9.

B 4

a rude to all my friends when I invite them round to our flat?
b promise not to play such loud music in the evenings.
c get to class late again. Honestly.
d be there on time – for once!
e and obey you forever.
f but you have to organise the drinks.
g if you'll do all the cooking.
h but I don't promise to make a particularly good job of it.
i the bathroom tidy, at least?
j you'll never misbehave in class again?

B 5
The sound changes from /aɪ/ to /ɑː/ because the pronunciation of *will* /wɪl/ changes to /l/.

C 2
a day, break, away, make, take
b cow, down, round, out, about
c so, go

C 3
a I promise I'll be at your house by four o'clock.
b I promise I'll be at your house by four o'clock.
c I promise I'll be at your house by four o'clock.
d I promise I'll be at your house by four o'clock.
e I promise I'll be at your house by four o'clock.

C 4
1 d
2 a
3 e
4 b
5 c

UNIT 8

A 1
a drop
b paint
c put up
d let
e make
f listen to
g ride
h have
i light
j drive
k use
l smoke

A 2
Light sometimes takes an object – see meaning 1. We know this because it says [T] (T = transitive). Sometimes it doesn't take an object – see meaning 2. We know this because it says [I] (I = intransitive).
Paint sometimes take an object and sometimes doesn't. We know this because it says [I] (= *intransitive* – i.e. doesn't take an object) and [T] (= *transitive* – i.e. takes an object).
Shout sometimes takes an object and sometimes doesn't [I/T].

A 3
bring [A]
come [S]
colour [S]
drive [S]
drop [S]
enjoy [A] (except in a special informal spoken use)
fall [N]
open [S]

A 4
a Don't bring food into the library.
b Don't drop litter.
c Don't drive too fast.
d Don't put up posters.
e Don't light bonfires.
f Don't ride bicycles on the pavement.
g Don't use a mobile phone.
h Don't spray-paint the walls.

A 5
a D
b D
c S
d D
e S
f S
g D
h S
i S
j D

A 6
a Different syllables are stressed.
b Different syllables are stressed.
c –
d Different syllables are stressed.
e –
f –
g Different syllables are stressed; different sounds are used.
h –
i –
j Different sounds are used for the first syllable.

B 1
a Yes, certainly.
b No sir. I'm afraid taking photographs is strictly forbidden.
c No, sorry. We operate a 'no dogs' policy.
d I'd rather you didn't.
e Sure. Help yourself
f Not at all. We'd love to meet her.

B 2
Asking for permission: Can I sit here please/use my camera in here? Are dogs allowed? Is it OK/all right if I use my mobile phone in here? Do you mind if I bring my sister to the party?
Saying yes: Sure. Yes, certainly. Not at all.
Saying no: I'd rather you didn't. No, sorry. No sir.

B 3
a Do you ... you didn't
b Is it all ... forbidden
c Can ... Help
d you mind ... at all

B 4
a A: Are children allowed in here? B: Sure, of course.
b A: Is it OK if I take a photograph here? B: I'd rather you didn't.
c A: Is it all right if I bring my dog in here? B: Yes it's okay, but keep it quiet.
d A: Do you mind if I take some photographs? B: I'm afraid that's not possible.
e A: Can I bring my friend to the party? B: Sure. She's welcome to come.
f A: Can I take one of these programmes? B: Sure. Help yourself.

C 2
fine – library, liar – bonfire, fear – here

C 3
Example answers
You dropped litter on the pavement.
You spray-painted the walls.
You put up posters everywhere.
You let your dog foul the footpath.
You made a lot of noise at night.
You rode your bicycle on the pavement.
You have an over-sensitive car alarm.
You lit a smoky bonfire.
You drove too fast in a built-up area.
You used your mobile phone on the train.
You smoked in a public place.

C 4
List 1: amazing, exactly, forbidden, graffiti, occasion, opinion, permission
List 2: certainly, sensitive, signature

UNIT 9

A 1
a Yes. We know because the verb is transitive [T].
b *fists*, *teeth* and *jaw*

A 2
a clench (fist, teeth)
b cross (arms, fingers, legs)
c fold (arms)
d nod (head)
e point (finger)
f raise (eyebrows, hand)
g scratch (ear, head)
h shake (arm, finger, fist, hands)
i shrug (shoulders)
j wag (finger)
k wave (arms, hand)

A 3
a John.
b Pete.
c The dog.
d Simon.
e Sarah.
f Sasha.
g Mel.
h Terry.
i Carl.
j Maisie.

A 4
a shaking his fist
b nodding her head
c pointing his finger
d shrugging her shoulders
e crossing his legs
f waving his hand
g shaking her finger
h scratching his/her head
i raising her eyebrows
j folding her arms

A 5
a different (two syllables)
b interest (two syllables)
c usually (three syllables)

d consciously (three syllables)
e general (two syllables)
f intimacy (four syllables)
g subconsciously (four syllables)
h relaxation (four syllables)

A 6

Example answers

a determined, dictionary, comfortable
b collocation, disagreement, indifference

B 1

a **1** It's difficult to say **2** shake your fist **3** Anything else **4** fold your arms
b **1** do this scene **2** easy to say **3** what do I do **4** folding your arms **5** shrug your shoulders

B 2

Asking for advice: How do you want me to do this scene? What do I do? What do you recommend? Anything else?

Expressing doubt: It's difficult to say. That's not easy to say.

Giving advice: I think you can come in and ... I think you can show boredom by ... Well you could fold your arms ... Well you could shrug your shoulders ...

Checking you have understood correctly: Is this what you had in mind? Like this?

Agreeing with an action: Yes, that's the kind/type of thing.

B 3

a want
b think
c mind
d think
e Anything
f easy
g type/kind
h could
i could

B 4

a else?
b to say.
c me to play this scene?
d scratch your ear or something.
e this?
f and cross your legs.
g the kind of thing.
h would show you are relaxed.

B 5

Actor: How do you want me to play this scene?
Director: It's difficult to say. I reckon you could scratch your ear or something.
Actor: Like this?
Director: Yes, that's the kind of thing.
Actor: Anything else?
Director: Well yes. You could sit down and cross your legs. That would show you are relaxed.

C 1

Possible answers

arm, cross, finger, fold, head, nod, raise, scratch, shake, wag, wave

C 2

a 1 4 sounds: /k - r - ɒ - s/
2 5 sounds: /f - ɪ - ŋ - g - ə/
3 9 sounds: /ɪ - n - d - ɪ - f - r - ə - n - s/
4 5 sounds: /p - ʌ - z - l - d/
5 8 sounds: /s - t - r - əɪ - n - dʒ - ə - z/
6 4 sounds: /t - r - uː - θ/
b intimacy, relaxation, subconsciously

C 3

a 6
b 7
c 3
d 4
e 9
f 8
g 2
h 5
i 1

UNIT 10

A 1

calculator	c
computer	n
contact lenses	g
credit card	d
hearing aid	j
electric guitar	q
electric toothbrush	a
electronic personal organiser	e
keyboard	o
microwave oven	h
mobile phone	l
monitor	k
mouse	p
personal stereo	b
printer	f
scanner	m
television	i

A 2

a go online
b emails
c website
d crashes
e computer viruses
f bug

A 3

a Five
b Sometimes it is countable (it says [C] in the dictionary) and sometimes it is uncountable (it says [U] in the dictionary).
c for, to do
d Meaning 3 is used when talking about computers (the dictionary says *computing*). Meaning 4 is a rather formal word (it says 'formal' in the dictionary).

A 4

a Switch on the computer, the monitor and the printer.
b Open the application you want.
c Work.
d Save your work on to the hard disk.
e Print your work.
f Close the application.
g Switch off the computer, the monitor and the printer.

B 1

do you know how to connect up to the Internet? b1
Have you checked the connection a2
How may I help you? c1
No. Do you think that will help? a3
OK. I'll give it a try. c3
Really? c2
Thanks. That's great! b2
Well, I can't get my personal organiser to work with my computer. a1

B 2

a Can you help me? Do you know how to connect up to the Internet? This thing is driving me crazy.
b Have you checked the batteries? Just click on the icon. That's what I would do. The best thing to do is to switch off and start again. Why don't you try and see? What seems to be the problem?
c Do you think that will help? OK. I'll give it a try. Really? Thanks. That's great.

B 3

The woman speaks more fluently.

B 4

a Can you help me?
b What seems to be the problem?
c Have you checked the batteries?
d Do you know how to use this answerphone?
e What is the problem?
f What do I do now?

B 6

a Sure. Just press the red button and record your message.
b Well, that's what I would do.
c The best thing would be to call the garage.
d Is it plugged in?
e You're welcome.
f Why? What seems to be the problem?

B 7

a Can
b problem
c sure
d know
e click
f happens
g at
h get
i crazy
j Have
k what
l don't
m thing
n start
o switched
p been

C 1
Words connected with computers: computer, computer bug, computer virus, crash (of a computer), disk, emails, go online, hard disk, keyboard, modem, monitor, printer, scanner, the computer's crashed, website

C 2
a column 1: electric, computer
column 2: personal, microwave, monitor, stereo
column 3: television, electronic
column 4: organiser, calculator
b column 1: credit, microwave, crashed
column 2: disk, scanner
column 3 : electric, electronic

C 3
a Thank you.
b Thank you.
c Thanks a lot.
d Thank you very much.
e Thank you very much for your help.
f No problem.
g Don't mention it.
h Glad I could help.

UNIT 11

A 1
a 4
b 3
c 2
d 1

A 2
a a sculpture
b based on a
c set in
d about
e the story

A 3
a 5
b 2
c 4, 8
d 7
e 1
f 3, 6
g The questions 1, 2, 3, 5 and 7 could be used for books too.

A 4
a comic ... comedy
b romance ... romantic comedies
c tragedy
d musical
e opera
f detective
g thrillers
h science
i westerns
j war
k horror
l action
m autobiography ... biography
n historical
o animated

A 5
a The American pronunciation includes a final /r/.
b of
c It is uncountable.

A 6
a What's your favourite Bond film?
b What are the best bits in the film?
c Who's in it?
d What part does Halle Berry play in the film?
e What kind of film is it?
f Who are the main characters in the film?
g What's the story of the film?

B 1
a You must have been really fed up.
b That can't have been much fun.
c You must have been pleased.

B 2
a wonderful
b exhausted
c been easy
d hurt yourself
e much fun

B 3
Example answers
a That must have been fantastic!
b That can't have been pleasant.
c You must have been tired.
d That can't have been easy.
e That must have been frightening!
f You must have been excited!
g You must have been delighted!
h That can't have been very nice.

B 4
a 6
b 2
c 1
d 5
e 9
f 4
g 10
h 8
i 3
j 7

B 5
a A: How was the film?
B: Fantastic.
A: Fantastic?
B: Fantastic!
b A: How long do you think the film was?
B: An hour and a half?
A: Ha!
B: Two hours?
A: Ha!
B: Two and a half hours?
A: Keep going.
B: Three hours?
A: Three and a half hours.
B: Three and a half hours?!
A: Yes.
B: No!
A: Yes. Three and a half hours.
B: Three and a half hours!

B 6
It was the intonation the speakers used.

C 2
a /g/: autobiography, biography
/dʒ/: logical, tragedy
b 1 autobiography
2 animated, biography

C 3
a You might have hurt yourself.
b You can't have been very pleased.
c That must have been terrifying.
d You could have been in real danger.
e That couldn't have been pleasant.

UNIT 12

A 1
a head: ear, eye, nose, tooth
b neck: throat
c shoulder: collar bone
d arm: elbow, wrist
e torso: stomach, waist
f hand: index finger, little finger, thumb
g leg: ankle, knee, thigh
h foot: heel, toes, big toe
i He's hurt his ankle/foot.

A 2
a adjective (*adj* in the dictionary)
b a river or stream
c They think they are cleverer, better etc. than they really are.

A 3
a headache, earache, toothache, stomach ache
b 1 broken nose/tooth/collar bone/arm/wrist/finger/thumb/ankle/leg/foot/toe
2 fractured collar bone/wrist/finger/leg/ankle/toe
3 sprained wrist/finger/ankle
4 swollen head/ear/nose/arm/elbow/wrist/finger/thumb/leg/ankle/knee/foot/heel/toe
5 sore head/ear/eye/throat/shoulder/arm/elbow/wrist/finger/thumb/leg/ankle/knee/foot/heel/toe
6 a pain in the neck

A 4
a She's got a stomach ache.
b He's got a swollen finger.
c She's got a broken leg.
d He's got a sprained ankle.
e She's got (a) toothache.
f He's got a broken nose.
g She's got a sore throat.
h He's got a swollen knee.
i She's got a headache.
j He's got a pain in his neck.
k She's got a broken finger.

A 5
(Look at the audioscript for Track 57, on page 88.)

B 1
a 2
b 6
c 1

d 3
e 4
f 5

B 2
a How are you? You're looking well. You look terrible. How about you? + 4, 12
b Fine. I'm fine. I had an infection. I'm better now. I've been a bit under the weather. + 1, 3, 5, 6, 7, 8, 9
c Good. Poor you. + 2, 10, 11, 13

B 3
a a bad back, flu, a migraine, a stomach ache, food poisoning, a cold
b ill, sick, terrible, not very well, off-colour

B 4
a how
b great
c wasn't
d problem/matter
e bed
f sorry
g broken
h playing
i about
j well
k let's

C 2
a *toe* is the odd one out. The others all have the sound /uː/ – tooth.
b *tooth* is the odd one out. The others all have the sound /əʊ/ – broken.

C 3
Example answers
a uncle
b some
c gain/paid
d land/sand
e rose/note
f missed/kissed
g more

C 4
a shoulder
b toes
c I'd give it to him
d If you rang home
e three tickets

UNIT 13

A 1
a 6
b 11
c 4
d 8
e 9
f 7
g 5
h 2
i 3
j 1
k 10

A 3
a composer
b manager
c singer
d cellist
e footballer
f chess player
g photographer
h teacher
i receptionist

A 4
a mathematics
b photograph
c piano
d saxophone
e biology
f therapy
g trombone
h violin
i reception
j journal

A 5
a mathematician D
b photographer D
c pianist D
d saxophonist D
e biologist S
f therapist S
g trombonist S
h violinist S
i receptionist S
j journalist S

A 6
a athlete
b pianist
c actor
d footballer
e drummer
f saxophonist
g cellist
h scientist
i receptionist
j composer
k guitarist

B 1
[1] How was the exam?
[6] You didn't have to do it!
[2] It was terrible.
[5] Oh, come on! I'm sure it wasn't that bad.
[3] Why? What happened?
[4] I couldn't answer one of the questions. I made a real mess of it.

B 2
a It was great.
b It went really well.
c I think it went OK.
d It wasn't too bad.
e It could have been worse.
f I couldn't think what to say/write.
g Horrible.
h I made a real mess of it.
i Absolutely terrible.

B 3
a BN
b GN
c BN
d BN
e BN
f BN
g GN
h GN
i BN

B 4
a 6
b 4
c 8
d 2
e 5
f 7
g 1
h 3

C 2
a /ɪ/ like *sit*
b /iː/ like *see*
c /aɪ/ like *light*

C 3
a receptionist
b percussion
c saxophone
d violin

C 4
a audience, interview, manager, songwriter, therapist
b conductor, remember,
c engineer
d photographer